# Mothering Ourselves

*Also by the author*

*Mothers and Daughters: Loving and Letting Go*

# Mothering Ourselves

## Help and Healing for Adult Daughters

Evelyn Silten Bassoff, Ph.D.

A DUTTON BOOK

DUTTON
Published by the Penguin Group
Penguin Books USA Inc., 375 Hudson Street,
New York, New York 10014, U.S.A.
Penguin Books Ltd, 27 Wrights Lane,
London W8 5TZ, England
Penguin Books Australia Ltd, Ringwood,
Victoria, Australia
Penguin Books Canada Ltd, 2801 John Street,
Markham, Ontario, Canada L3R 1B4
Penguin Books (N.Z.) Ltd, 182–190 Wairau Road,
Auckland 10, New Zealand

Penguin Books Ltd, Registered Offices:
Harmondsworth, Middlesex, England

First published by Dutton, an imprint of New American Library,
a division of Penguin Books USA Inc.
Distributed in Canada by McClelland & Stewart Inc.

First Printing, January, 1991
10 9 8 7 6 5 4 3 2 1

REGISTERED TRADEMARK—MARCA REGISTRADA

LIBRARY OF CONGRESS CATALOGING IN PUBLICATION DATA
Bassoff, Evelyn.
    Mothering ourselves : help and healing for adult daughters / by
Evelyn Silten Bassoff.
        p.   cm.
    ISBN 0-525-24938-9
    1. Mothers and daughters—United States.   2. Motherhood—United
States—Psychological aspects.   I. Title.
HQ755.85.B364   1991
306.874'3—dc20                                                90-19427
                                                                   CIP

Printed in the United States of America
Set in Palatino
Designed by Kathryn Parise

*To my colleagues in the Tuesday group:*
Lyn Gullette, Katharine Krueger, Ivan Miller,
Wayne Phillips, Susan Rosewell-Jackson,
Carol E. Ryan, and Don Williams
*With Gratitude*


And to my husband, Bruce,
*With Love*

# ACKNOWLEDGMENTS

I would like to thank my clients, who have trusted me with their personal stories and whose experiences inform every chapter of this book. By sharing their joys, hurts, failures, and triumphs, they have enlarged my understanding and greatly enriched my life.

Heartfelt thanks go to my family. My husband, Bruce, carefully followed the development of the manuscript and offered invaluable editorial assistance; moreover, he fostered my courage to go deep within and write what is true for me rather than what might please others or conform to their standards. My mother, Helene Frank Silten, also encouraged my honesty, when, rather than holding me back from looking with wide-open eyes at our relationship (as a less generous, more defensive woman might have done), she gave me her blessings to explore and freely write about it. I am grateful as well to my in-laws, Sylvia and Isidore Bassoff, for their genuine interest in my work. And although my children, Jon and Leah, were not directly involved in this project, their loving presence deepens the meaning of everything I do.

I am indebted to Elaine Koster, Senior Vice President and Publisher at Dutton, for her unhesitant support of my work and to Alexia Dorszynski, Senior Editor, for her wise editorial counsel as well as her encouragement, kindness, and availability. Special thanks are due my long-time friend Alice Levine, who copyedited and proofread the manuscript with sensitivity and meticulous care. I am also grateful to the administration of the University of Colorado in Boulder for providing secretarial assistance; Sue Middleton and Suzanne Reissig of the School of Education were most responsive.

Many people in the mental health community made significant contributions. Dr. John P. Haws provided early direction and inspiration. Without my asking, Dr. Lee Moyers, Helen Flanders, and Don Williams presented me with books and journal articles that proved to be enormously useful. Colleagues in a monthly discussion group—Katharine Krueger, Don Willliams, and Drs. Lyn Gullette, Ivan Miller, Wayne Phillips, Susan Rosewell-Jackson, and Carol E. Ryan—offered needed encouragement and substantive suggestions throughout the writing process; I am deeply and forever touched by their unfailing regard.

My appreciation also goes to new and old friends and colleagues: Julie Phillips for reviewing the manuscript with expert care and providing new insights; Professor Siegfried Mandel for trying to locate the source of an obscure quote; Ben Eilbott, my first mentor, for spending much time (and a shameful amount of money) on a long-distance call in order to help me untangle an intellectual knot; and Geri Cassens, Katharine Krueger, Alice Levine, Susan Rosewell-Jackson, and Eleanor Mimi Schrader, my closest women friends, for nurturing me in countless ways.

Thank you all.

—Evelyn S. Bassoff

# CONTENTS

# INTRODUCTION

# *The Lost Mother*

I must be very young; my mother is still singing,
all the time; I gaze at her fine, pink face, glowing
in the window light. Her dark hair has small, tight
tight waves. They glow in the light. Everything
glows. I am aglow with the rapture of the revelation that she is the most beautiful in the whole
world, my mother.

—Adele Wiseman
*Old Woman at Play*

When my son and daughter were still small and
eager for bedtime stories, they liked me to tell them the story
of the lost mother. In the story a little country girl accom-
panies her mother to the market in a nearby village. Distracted by the colorful wares and the hustle and bustle of
the crowd, the child gets separated from her mother, and
although she looks everywhere, cannot find the missing
woman. Quite beside herself—for can anything be worse
than losing one's mother?—she wanders over to the village
square and, sobbing bitterly, seeks solace in the shade of an
oak tree. Luckily, a sympathetic soldier comes across the
frightened child, calms her down, and promises to help her.
When he asks the little girl to describe her lost mother, the
girl's unhappy face breaks into a great smile. "My mother
is surely the most beautiful and kindest woman in all the
world. You will not have any difficulty recognizing her," she
says. With this, the soldier sets out toward the crowded
marketplace to begin his search. It is not long before he
comes upon a lady of singular beauty and refined demeanor.

Confident that he has found the child's mother, he insists, against her vigorous protest, that she accompany him to the place where his little charge waits. But upon seeing the beauty, the poor child bursts into tears, for the stranger is certainly not her mother. Despite his frustration, the kind soldier tries to soothe the disappointed child and also apologize to the beautiful lady for imposing on her when, seemingly out of the blue, a very homely looking woman comes charging toward the threesome. Wagging a finger at the little girl, she sharply scolds her for having gotten lost and being such a trouble to everyone. Shamed by this tongue-lashing, the child begs to be forgiven, then throws her arms around the angry woman and cries out, "But, oh, Mommy, how happy I am to be with you again."

Like the child in this story, we too, when very young, saw our mother through rose-colored glasses. However flawed she may have been in reality, to us she was the kindest and most beautiful person in the world. Because we were helpless and little and our well-being depended on her care and love, we needed to believe in her goodness, so we endowed her with a beautiful nature: a selfless, wise, and constant love for us. Consequently, when she acted without tenderness or empathy or fairness, we did not blame her. Needing her so much, we were less threatened by believing that we—rather than she—were somehow defective and therefore deserving of her unkindness. To ensure we could feel safe in her good hands, we protected her perfect image even at the expense of tarnishing our self-image.

One of the rude awakenings of adulthood is the realization that our mothers were not always good to us. For most of us this means accepting mother's human limitations and shortcomings. As the delightful young heroine in the movie *Days of Heaven* reminds us, "Nobody's *poyfict.*" Even a well-meaning mother cannot be always available or in harmony with the needs of her child, and even a mother with the best intentions will make mistakes. In fact, our mothers' human limitations and shortcomings fostered our growth and development; had they behaved infallibly, they would have stunted us. Frustrated by mother's imperfect love, we were forced to become resilient, to make do, to get around obstacles—in short, to adapt to our imperfect world.

But for others among us, the awakening is ruder. It means coming to grips with the knowledge that the person to whom we entrusted our lives failed us in significant ways, leaving us frustrated, hurt, and angry—leaving us wounded.

Confronting the deficiencies in our mothers and the hurt they inflicted generates enormous discomfort. No longer believing that our childhood was happy and sheltered, we may come to feel like orphans abandoned in a cold world. As one of my psychotherapy clients, a college student, put it, "But if my own mother didn't love me—which is what I'm beginning to suspect—will anyone ever love me? Will anyone care about me? What is to become of me?"

Feeling betrayed by the mother of our childhood, we may succumb to a terrible anger—a rage that writer Louise Bernikow, upon recognizing the glaring weakness of her own mother, describes as "raw and riotous, embarrassing in its power."[1] Or we may be consumed by a silent, slow-growing anger. During a therapy session, a soft-spoken woman in her late thirties tells me, "Now that I am aware that my mother knew about her boyfriend's sexual advances toward me when I was a child and chose not to protect me against him, I am finding it increasingly painful to be in her presence. I cannot even pick up the telephone to say hello to her. Inside me is a *swelling* anger."

Knowing that we have been deprived of the full gift of motherlove, we may experience shame. For example, the timorous twenty-year-old daughter of a mother who had committed suicide when the daughter was two told me that she found herself glaring enviously at the carefree, giggling young women who patronized the dress shop where she worked. She confided that she hated them because it was so obvious that, unlike her, they had been loved. She fantasized that these strangers intuitively knew she was motherless and, by virtue of this fact, "defective." "I sometimes imagine that when people look at me what they see is nothing but a shell of a person—a bombed-out building—and I often ask myself what's wrong with me that my mother abandoned me.''

Almost always the awareness that our mothers did not care for us well enough precipitates depression. As we lose the hope of the wise, unselfish, unconditionally loving mother, we feel shaky and insecure and diminished. I am reminded of the achingly sad words of Tillie Olsen's character Clara as she stands by the deathbed of the mother who had remained remote and inaccessible to her:

> Where did we lose each other, first mother, singing mother?
> Annulled the quarrels, the gibing, the harshness between; the fall into silence and the withdrawal.
> I do not know you, Mother. Mother, I never knew you.[2]

Although coming to grips with the fact that our mothers may have failed us in significant ways and that our childhoods were less than happy unlooses dark feelings—abandonment, anger, rage, shame, and loss—confronting our past ultimately helps us become well and, in the best circumstances, encourages us to be more compassionate human beings. In the cherishing language of a lover, the poet W. H. Auden once addressed his inner pain—his woundedness—as a gift and thanked it for the insight it bestowed on him. "Knowing you," he said, "has made me understand."[3] To be sure, scratching away the layers of scar tissue that have formed over an unclean wound causes a piercing pain, but until the festering motherwound is exposed to the light, it cannot heal properly.

One of my major purposes in writing *Mothering Ourselves* is to help adult daughters uncover their unhealed motherwounds and to expose them to the good light of understanding. In Chapters 1 through 4, we will look at the failures of our childhood mothers—particularly failures of empathy, nurturance and protection, and separation (letting go)—and we will consider the ways these failures still affect us as adult daughters. We will also explore the relationship between the mother's failure to realize her life—that is, to become a full person in her own right—and our fears as adult daughters to lay claim to our lives.*

As my ideas for this book began to take shape, I presented them to a group of colleagues with whom I meet monthly for discussions, and although the group as a whole responded enthusiastically, one colleague startled me with her sharp criticism.

"Why in heaven's name do you want to write about the ways mothers have failed their daughters?" she asked. "Haven't mothers been everybody's scapegoats long enough? Do you really think it will do a grown-up woman any good to know that when she was little her 'developing self' was being damaged by her unattuned mother? Tell me, isn't it time for daughters to celebrate what is good between them and their mothers instead of harping on what is bad?"

"Yes, but . . ." I stumbled, unprepared for my colleague's onslaught.

"I have the uneasy feeling, Evi," she continued, "that by 'exposing,' as you put it, the crimes committed in the nursery, you'll be undermining the chances for mothers and daughters to make a good relationship with each other in the present. *You'll be opening a Pandora's Box.*"

After the meeting, I could not get my colleague's hard words out of my mind. Would this book be destructive, as she warned? Should I scratch this project?

A few days later, without knowing exactly why, I decided to research the origins of Pandora's Box. I discovered that

---

* The fact that I have written about the difficulties between mothers and daughters does not imply that the relationship between fathers and daughters is unimportant. For better and for worse, fathers profoundly affect their daughters' lives; like mothers, they have the capacity to wound and to bless. Moreover, the father's role in the family—whether he is nurturant or uninvolved, supportive or undermining—affects the ways his wife mothers as well as the well-being of the family. I have chosen to focus on the mother-daughter relationship not out of disregard for other family relationships, but because it is, in itself, a vast and complicated subject—one I have studied for over ten years in my capacities as psychologist and university professor.

in one version, Pandora's Box held all the human miseries, which, with the exception of Hope, flew forth when the box was opened by the god Epimetheus; but that in another version, the box—or more accurately a honey-vase or womb-symbol like a cornucopia—contained all the blessings of the gods. The discrepant descriptions of the contents of Pandora's Box suggested to me that distinctions between human miseries and human blessings are not absolute, that bad and good are somehow connected, and, in fact, that one can become the other.

As my colleague correctly noted, indulging in the ugly sport of mother-blaming could only be destructive. Like the foolish god Epimetheus, I would be thoughtless if I simply let loose all the old miseries between mothers and daughters. Although I strongly believe that exposing the hurts, anger, disappointments, and frustrations between mothers and daughters is a necessary *first step* in the healing process, I agree with my colleague that it is not enough. My colleague's challenge led me to define another major purpose of *Mothering Ourselves:* to help adult daughters transform what was hurtful and damaging during their childhoods into something new and good and hopeful, just as many of my clients have been able to change their miseries into blessings.

Hence, Chapters 6 through 8 of *Mothering Ourselves* focus on ways we wounded adult daughters can soothe and ultimately transcend our pain, take what was miserable and destructive and change it into something vital and positive. In these chapters, we will explore many pathways toward well-being. We will look at different kinds of reparative human relationships—both in and out of the therapeutic setting—and consider how they can compensate for missed motherlove. We will also look at nonhuman sources of healing: the practice of solitude, connections with nature, and engagement in creative activities.

In Chapter 9, we will return to our mothers in an effort to complete the healing process. Having come to terms with what went wrong between us and them, we will now be better prepared to affirm what is good and, in the most fortunate circumstances, to bridge the chasms that separated us from them.

In writing *Mothering Ourselves*, I draw from a rich and diverse literature in psychology—particularly the works of Heinz Kohut and Alice Miller. But because I am a wanderer, I have not been content to stay put among the reknowned thinkers of my field. Novelists and poets have lured me, and the writings of Virginia Woolf, Colette, Toni Morrison, Vivian Gornick, Tillie Olsen, May Sarton, and Maurice Sendak inform my understanding of the mother-daughter relationship as much as those of the great psychologists. Ancient myths, fairy tales, and folktales also pull me from scientific books because in childhood stories I always seem to discover wonderful insights regarding human behavior and relationships. Indeed, Chapter 5 is an interpretation of *The Wizard of Oz*, and Dorothy Gale, the little girl from Kansas, is a central character throughout the last chapters.

In sorting through the complexities of the mother-daughter experience, I also turn to my personal experiences as daughter and granddaughter. Because writing *Mothering Ourselves* is a healing journey for me, I have chosen to share my hurts, frustrations, and growth in the hope that readers can identify with and even benefit from my struggles.

However, as was true in my first book, *Mothers and Daughters: Loving and Letting Go*, the personal stories of my clients are the real heart and soul of this book.[4] Many women who have suffered maternal deprivations have shared their stories with me. Listening to them, I have learned a great deal about human nature.

To my sorrow, I have known some women so beaten down by their experiences that they lacked the hope and energy to turn things around for themselves. I recall one client, for example, a bright and restless woman battered by her paranoid schizophrenic mother since infancy, who seemed to create one crisis after another for herself: doomed relationships with battering men, failures at work. I saw this client for only three sessions, after which time she terminated treatment and returned to the abusive boyfriend she had left for a month. Along with her payment for my services was a short note: "Thanks anyway—but it's too little, too late." That she gave up—at least during the time I knew her—disappointed but did not surprise me; her spirit had been exhausted.

What has surprised and exhilarated me again and again, however, is that other clients with grim personal histories have somehow triumphed. Time and again these women remind me that with courage, tenacity, and inventiveness, we can heal the motherwound. Like the little village girl who was distraught when she lost her mother, we as small children depended absolutely on the loving and wise care of our mothers. But, as adult daughters, we have more resources. What they have not been able to provide, we can find in other places and make our own.

# PART I

 *Woundings*

When I was a child, I had a recurring fantasy that was so powerful, it was almost hallucinatory. I would imagine that I heard someone crying, and this crying was so poignant, so compelling, that I would start to leap up from my bed each time to try to find that person and take care of her. I had no idea until much later in life that the crying was part of myself . . .

—Kathie Carlson
*In Her Image: The Unhealed Daughter's Search for Her Mother*

# CHAPTER 1

## *Mother to Daughter: Distortions, Disapproval, and Disregard*

I require a You to become; becoming I, I say You.
—Martin Buber
*I and Thou*

Several years ago, at the start of psychotherapy, I had a terrible dream. I was in a railroad station with a ticket home to mother, but I had so many trunks, suitcases, and boxes that I could hardly move toward the track where the trains departed. Frantically, I pushed and pulled my unwieldy load, when, to my shame, the bags split open, spilling out the ripped and soiled underclothes of a child. Red-faced, glancing furtively about to make sure no one noticed my humiliation, I tried to stuff the scattered clothing back into the suitcases; but, despite my efforts, I could not get them shut.

With my therapist's guidance, I was able to decipher the meaning of the dream. It revealed that before I could get "on track" and return to my mother in a meaningful way, I needed to confront our shared past: to look at the contents of the baggage that I had lugged about for years. At first I resisted my therapist's direction—going over all that childhood "stuff" *again* seemed unnecessary—but she was insistent. So, taking her hand, I embarked on a journey that proved to be long and arduous but ultimately healing.

Just as I turned to a therapist for guidance and comfort,

women now come to me for help. They too seldom initiate therapy to explore early problems with mother; rather they present troubled relationships with lovers or husbands or problems at work or feelings of inadequacy, loneliness, emptiness, and anxiety. What frequently happens, however, is that after a few sessions, whatever the presenting problem might have been, their attention turns to mother. As they talk about less-than-happy childhoods, they begin to connect their present distress to her early influence. Whether we like this fact or not, the ways our mothers—who, in almost all cases, were our primary caretakers—responded to us when we were in their charge affect us still. And whatever our age—whether we are sixteen or sixty—we want to believe our mothers loved us wisely, generously, and unselfishly. As psychotherapy progresses, I am often witness to the anger and despair of clients as they come to understand that their mothers' love was flawed—often significantly so. Nevertheless, I am convinced that understanding what went wrong between us and them is a necessary part of healing.

One of the most significant problems of early maternal care involves failures on the part of the mother to resonate, or be in tune, with what her child feels. A mother must recognize happiness, fear, confusion, frustration—the whole range of human emotion—to understand and respond to her child with empathy and genuine love. Every child needs to be *mirrored*—to have her inner experiences acknowledged and, as psychiatrist Heinz Kohut puts it, "to be looked upon with joy and basic approval by a delighted parent."[1] When, for example, the baby crawls out of mother's lap toward the toys at the far end of the room, she will look back to check that mother is still there. But she will also seek to confirm that mother is sharing the suspense, scariness, and wonder of her adventure. The exuberance in mother's voice ("Wow! Look at baby go! Look at the pretty toys baby has found!"), the glimmer in her eyes, the vibrations of her body all affirm the child's experience, allowing her to feel *real*. Similarly, when the crying child who has just bumped against the table's edge and bruised her chin feels mother's sweet kiss and hears her sympathetic words, "There, there, that must have hurt," she knows her own pain and tears are valid.

The need to be mirrored accurately and lovingly is most urgent during our early formative years. When we are very young we require our mother's full attention and her absolute adoration. As author Nancy Friday says, the baby must have the best seat—the only seat!—at the Adoration Banquet. If our baby needs are met, we are filled with the knowledge of our essential goodness and, as we get older, we are able to relinquish the unrealistic demand to be the focus of mother's life and the most important person on earth.

When a woman is less than adequate as a parent, she does not reflect and celebrate her child *as she is;* instead she *consistently* ignores or misinterprets her child's feelings. In the following excerpt from psychoanalyst Daniel N. Stern's *The Interpersonal World of the Infant,* we see how a mother with too little empathy, much like the distorting mirrors in a house of horrors, may actually twist and reshape her infant's self-perception.

Molly's mother was very controlling. She had to design, initiate, direct, and terminate all agendas. She determined which toy Molly should play with, how Molly was to play with it ("Shake it up and down—don't roll it on the floor"), when Molly was done playing with it, and what to do next ("Oh, here is Dressy Bessy. Look!"). The mother overcontrolled the interaction to such an extent that it was often hard to trace the natural crescendo and decrescendo of Molly's own interest and excitement. . . . Molly found an adaptation. She gradually became more compliant. Instead of actively avoiding or opposing these intrusions, she became one of those enigmatic starers into space. . . . This general dampening of her affectivity continued . . . and was still apparent at three years . . .[2]

One might say that Molly's mother, unable to join with and appreciate her child's unique experience, robbed the little one of her own feelings. Molly seems to have developed what child psychiatrist Donald W. Winnicott coined "the false self," the self that complies with others' wishes at the expense of losing its vitality. In my practice, I counsel a young woman who is a grown-up version of Molly. She tells me that she is unsure of her own experience.

I go to a movie or to a play, but I don't know how I feel about it. Instead of my own thoughts, I hear my mother's voice in my head telling me if the acting was good, if the plot held up. I take what I think my mother would think and make it mine.

As a consequence of her mother's consistent failure to mirror her accurately, the child misses the vital experience of being affirmed, admired, appreciated, seen, heard, understood, and known as she is. In extreme cases, if the mother is generally unresponsive, the unreflected daughter may feel that she has no inner self.[3] Just as the philosopher poses the age-old question, "If no one hears the falling tree crash in the forest, has it made a sound?" this child asks herself, "If no one knows who I am, am I real?"

Andrea, a former client, described an incident that illuminates the experience of being unrecognized and therefore feeling unreal to herself. When she was in the fourth grade, Andrea won first place in a school-wide spelling bee. Bursting with pride, she ran all the way home, ready to share her exciting news with her mother. However, she found her alcoholic mother in a dazed stupor.

I wanted her to be proud of me. I blurted out the wonderful news, then waited expectantly for some kind of recognition. But when I looked at her, what I saw was so awful. Her blue eyes were murky and glazed over and seemed to me like the dead eyes of the fish she would serve up on Friday nights. Suddenly, my prize didn't matter any more. Winning first place meant nothing. I felt like a nothing.

Unrecognized by her mother, Andrea was *drained* of her own experience. Andrea's story reminds me of another. Years ago I taught fourth grade in New York City. One of my pupils, ordinarily a well-behaved little girl, would become suddenly agitated during quiet times. For example, when her best girlfriend was reading silently or had her head on her desk for a rest period, Darlene would tickle her, pull at her clothes, yank her hair—do the most annoying things— to engage her. What I later learned was that from the time of Darlene's birth, Darlene's mother suffered from an immobilizing depression, which left her unable to interact with her children. I could easily imagine poor baby Darlene, desperate for recognition, tugging, pulling, and tearing at her mother. Could it be, I wondered, that when Darlene's girlfriend temporarily withdrew into her own space, Darlene was overcome with anxiety—the same feeling of being without a self she had known with her unresponsive mother?

Just as children turn to their mothers for recognition, so do grown women yearn for their mothers' basic approval and understanding. When our mothers delight in us, we are enhanced; when they disregard us, we are demoralized.

Beth, an assistant professor of literature, tells me that her mother often asks which books she's reading so that she can read them too. When they visit with one another, mother and daughter talk for hours on end about Beth's intellectual work.

My mother, at sixty-six, is still very much interested in me and my world. When we are pursuing ideas together, I feel valued and known; in her presence, I don't, for a minute, doubt the meaningfulness of my life.

Contrast Beth's experience with that of Carolyn: "I am still waiting for my mother to notice that I am a terrific single parent. I am still devastated because she withholds her approval." In a similar vein, Barbara confides,

> I bought myself a great-looking dress for my mother's seventieth birthday party. Ten minutes before the guests were to arrive, she looked me up and down with those critical eyes of hers and said, "Are you going to wear *that*?" Once again she had succeeded in making me feel ugly and wrong. At that instant I could have killed her. But it wasn't long before my anger at her dissipated and I fell into a depression.

Unlike Carolyn and Barbara, Riva tells me that her mother is not critical of her. The problem, however, is that this mother consistently fails to understand her daughter.

> When mother and I have a conversation, we are not connected. I tell her something and she responds with a comment or a question that is irrelevant. I am almost afraid to share anything personal with her because she trivializes it through her lack of understanding. So I shut down, hating her because she doesn't ever seem to "get it," because she seems so stupid to me. But then I hate myself for my intolerance.

The unmirrored daughter's alternating feelings of anger and depression that Barbara and Riva describe are also conveyed in a touching passage from Vivian Gornick's memoir, *Fierce Attachments*.

> Today is promising, tremendously promising. Wherever I go, whatever I see, whatever my eye or ear touches, the space radiates expansion. . . .
> I go to meet my mother. I'm flying. Flying! I want to give her some of this shiningness bursting in me, siphon in her my immense happiness at being alive. Just because

she is my oldest intimate and at this moment I love everybody, even her.

"Oh, Ma! What a day I've had," I say.

"Tell me," she says. "Do you have the rent this month?"

"Ma, listen . . ." I say.

"That review you wrote for the *Times*," she says. "It's
for sure they'll pay you?"

"Ma, stop it. Let me tell you what I've been feeling," I
say.

"Why aren't you wearing something warmer?" she cries.
"It's nearly winter."

The space inside begins to shimmer. The walls collapse
inward. I feel breathless. Swallow slowly, I say to myself,
slowly. To my mother I say, "You *do* know how to say the
right thing at the right time. It's remarkable, this gift of
yours. It quite takes my breath away."

But she doesn't get it. She doesn't know I'm being ironic.
Nor does she know she's wiping me out. She doesn't know
I take her anxiety personally, feel annihilated by her
depression. How can she know this? She doesn't even
know I'm there. Were I to tell her that it's death to me,
her knowing I'm there, she would stare at me out of her
eyes crowding up with puzzled desolation, this young girl
of seventy-seven . . .[4]

Of course, no human mother can *always* be warmly responsive to her daughter's experience, and, as is only natural, every mother will at times respond with disapproval,
frustration, impatience, confusion, and anger. Moreover, she
will withdraw her attentions when she is tired or distracted
or in the midst of her own thoughts. Paradoxically, the mother's imperfect responses—the misunderstandings, misinter-
pretations, and "tuning out" that are a part of all human
relationships—actually help the child to develop her inner
resources. Because her mother cannot meet all her needs,
the daughter must learn how to meet her own. As a result
she becomes more resourceful, supple, and able to adapt.

Moreover, the enhancing mother consciously sets limits

for her growing child and corrects her antisocial behaviors. Just as she recognizes her child's feelings, she does not allow her to trample on the rights of others—including her own. It is only as mother and child respect each other's differences and separateness that a *healthy relationship*, rather than a *merged attachment*, becomes possible. In a healthy relationship, each partner knows, "I am me and you are you. I cannot do with you as I like because you are not part of me. You cannot do with me as you like because I am not part of you."

In Toni Morrison's masterpiece *Beloved*, we see the grotesque consequences of a merged attachment between the mother Sethe, a former slave girl, and Beloved, the murdered baby daughter who mysteriously returns to her in the form of a young woman. Out of her terrible guilt for murdering her child, Sethe is determined to gratify Beloved's every wish and whim, as if she were a little baby. In the process, however, Sethe is depleted and becomes a mere wisp of the vital woman she once was, and Beloved is transformed into a greedy, human monster—a young woman who throws violent tantrums when she is denied, sleeps wherever she happens to be, and constantly whines for sweets although she is getting bigger and plumper by the day. It is Denver, Sethe's other daughter, who helplessly observes her family's gradual destruction.

> They grew tired, and even Beloved, who was getting bigger, seemed nevertheless as exhausted as they were. . . . Listless and sleepy with hunger Denver saw the flesh between her mother's forefinger and thumb fade. Saw Sethe's eyes bright but dead, alert but vacant, paying attention to everything about Beloved—her lineless palms, her forehead, the smile under the jaw, crooked and much too long—everything except her basket-fat stomach.[5]

Whatever our age, we long for and deserve mother's recognition and basic approval, but, as reasonable adults, we must accept that we are not the center of the universe. The grandiose Beloved—whose every whim is indulged by her mother and who knows no limits—is as out of control as is her unbounded, spreading body. Just as the poorly mirrored daughter is wounded, the daughter whose importance and sense of entitlement are magnified by mother is similarly disabled. She will always be disappointed because, unlike her overindulgent mother, the people she encounters in everyday life do not constantly celebrate and adore her. Moreover, knowing in her heart that she is not the extraordinary being her mother makes her out to be but nevertheless feeling compelled to act as if she is, she will feel fraudulent— she will have a "false self."

Our folklore is rich with superstitions and stories that depict the significance of being mirrored. For example, vampires, demons, and other imaginary soulless creatures do not have reflections. Although they masquerade as human beings, the absence of a mirror-image reveals their inferiority. Anthropologist Sir James George Frazer notes that primitive man and woman regarded their reflections and shadows as their very souls, and that when these images were trampled upon, stuck, or stabbed they would feel the injury as if it were done to their bodies. Because shattering the image of the self meant danger to one's soul, early societies also imposed severe taboos upon disturbing the water into which a person was gazing. Even today, some people entertain the superstition that breaking a mirror brings seven (the number symbolizing pain) years of bad luck.

The significance of the reflection-soul and the harmfulness of faulty maternal mirroring is poignantly described in the ancient Greek myth of Narcissus. In Ovid's famous version, written in A.D. 8, Narcissus, a beautiful but aloof young boy who spurns the attentions of the love-struck nymph Echo, falls in love with his own reflection. Eventually consumed by a terrible longing for himself, he gives up his life to become a little flower.

Although the parents of Narcissus (Liriope, the elusive

nymph, and Cipheus, the overpowering water god who rapes her) are little-known characters, they play an important part in their son's tragedy. Liriope is cold, nonmirroring, and self-involved—neither a goddess nor a human mother— while Cipheus is a crushing, invasive force.[6] The effects of their parental inaccessibility are touchingly expressed in a verse from a twelfth-century narrative poem, *Narcissus*, in which Narcissus expresses the hopelessness of his condition.

> I complain but none hears me. My parents know nothing of this. My friends have lost me. Why does not my mother know anything? If she came and grieved and wept over me it might give me some consolation, but no-one has seen me, then, who can bewail my beauty?[7]

Unmirrored, unseen, unreflected by his mother, Narcissus is cut off from his real self. Unlike the penetrating, loving eyes of a mother, which illuminate the child's true and whole self, the still water into which Narcissus obsessively peers can only reflect a superficial image. Not surprisingly, Narcissus, after whom Freud named the personality disturbance "narcissism," remains superficial: He is isolated, arrogant, friendless, and without compassion.

Echo's part in Narcissus's demise is also revealing. Although she is inflamed with love for him, she cannot heal his damaged being. Because of the spell cast by the vengeful goddess Saturnia, Echo loses the full use of her voice and is only able to repeat the last phrases of a speech. Consequently, her responses to Narcissus are partial, perfunctory, and hollow. Unable to clarify or interpret Narcissus's meanings, she can only flatter him by repeating part of what he says. Echo is, in the end, merely a pale copy of empathy; but Narcissus—and every person wounded by a nonmirroring parent—needs true empathy to heal.

I often see parallels between Narcissus's sad story and the lives of women I treat. When Bela first came to see me, she explained that her mother seemed supportive and loving but that in her presence, she nevertheless felt irritable, frustrated, and angry. Moreover, because her mother was always "nice," Bela could not understand the negative feelings that welled up inside, and she felt guilty for them. Only after several months of therapy could she acknowledge her mother's failings.

For as long as I can remember, my mother has told me how happy I am, how perfect my life is, how loving my husband and I are. But the truth is that I am prone to deep depressions, that my husband and I are burdened with myriad problems, and that our lives are far from perfect. Yet my mother will only see what is nice and undisturbing to her. Once when she visited us, she brought an assortment of doilies as a gift. She went about the house covering the stains on our old wooden tables and the worn-out backs of our upholstered chairs with these silly doilies. If she could, I suppose my mother would also cover me up with a doily so that my flaws are hidden from her eyes.

In therapy, Bela confided that as a child she had always withheld from her mother her fears, hurts, and disappointments by pretending to be the happy, adorable little girl her mother insisted on seeing. Like the tragic Narcissus, who saw nothing but his pretty face in the reflective pond, Bela, looking into her mother's eyes, would see only an acceptable version—her mother's version—of herself. Consequently, she felt like a part-person. She learned to hide from those around her and from herself the less pretty but normal parts of her personality: human emotions and feelings such as anger, jealousy, envy, and uncertainty. When she married and had a family, Bela believed that, like her, her husband and children had to appear perfect.

I fall apart if my husband makes a *faux pas* when we're out with friends. I am secretly resentful when my ten-year-old son messes up in Little League, or when my six-year-old daughter puts on a blouse and pants that clash. I can't help it, but I seem to need for them to be a certain way.

Bela's mother appeared to mirror her daughter, and to relatives and friends this cheerful woman seemed the ideal mother. On the surface, she was supportive, admiring, and appreciative. But, like Echo, her responses were shallow—nothing but empty words of flattery. It is reasonable to speculate that because she did not make the effort to understand and appreciate Bela in all her human complexity, Bela found it difficult to accept herself and her family members, whom she perceived as extensions of herself, when she and they were less than picture-perfect.

Partial recognition takes many forms and has various effects. For example, if mother joined with us only when we were buoyant and sunny but not when we were complaining or sad, we may, in turn, condemn ourselves for normal grievances and depressions: "What is wrong with me that I am feeling blue? Am I a wimp, a big baby?" Or, if mother was always responsive to our frail, sickly aspects but not to our vital and autonomous ones, we may hold back from life's adventures: "I think I'll pass on that horseback riding lesson and stay home to nurse my cold." A dear friend tells me that her mother, a successful scientist, was "always right there when it came to my intellectual growth, but turned away from me when I needed her to affirm my sensuality and sexuality as a young woman." Although my friend feels comfortable in her role as a top executive in a high-powered corporation, at thirty-five she is still painfully awkward whenever she dates a desirable man.

In an illuminating article, psychologist Richard A. Geist, who specializes in the treatment of eating disorders, provides clinical examples of what he calls "fragmented selfhood." He presents Penny, a twenty-year-old anorexic patient who recalls that when she dressed up for special occasions, she could not combine everything "so it felt like me" and that when she asked her mother how she looked her mother would always find something wrong: "You'd look fine if it weren't for your hair; let me fix it," or "Yes, dear, you look nice, but that necklace ruins the whole thing. I'll get you another." As Geist explains, Penny's mother could not allow her daughter to weave makeup, jewelry, clothes, and hairstyle into a unique motif. Instead, by substituting a hairstyle or necklace of her own choosing, she splintered her daughter's efforts to feel whole and *right*. In Geist's words,

> The anorexic girl peers into the mirror of the mother and perceives not the reflection of her whole body self, but a prismatic image of isolated parts: Her stomach protrudes, her thighs are fat; her birthmark is too noticeable. . . . Only when she allows mother to substitute the latter's "thing creation" does she feel whole and alive, and then only by sacrificing her uniqueness.[8]

A wonderful Norwegian folktale illustrates our need to be loved not for one part or another but for *all of us*. In this tale, a woman gives birth to twins; one twin is kind and sweet but the other, named Mophead, is quite a fright. Indeed, she is as unruly as her mop of wild, chaotic hair. The mother does not want to have anything to do with a child so embarrassingly loud and unconventional, but the angry Mophead insists on being who she is. When she finally is accepted by the prince who takes her as his bride, Mophead is transformed into a perfectly lovely girl.[9] The story teaches me that when those closest to us are sympathetic to *all of us*—our gentle side as well as our raging one, our buoyancy as well as our sadness, our intellect as well as our sensuality and sexuality—we cannot help but become lovable and loving.

I should like to point out that just as a daughter is blessed when her mother mirrors her with loving eyes, so is the mother blessed. In Yiddish there is a word that wonderfully describes such exhilaration: *Kvelling* is the trembling joy and awe of the parent as she beholds her child in all her unique, marvelous complexity.

Recently, I was deeply moved by an exchange with my elderly mother. After I had appeared on the Oprah Winfrey

Show to promote my first book, I sent a videotape of the program to her. Many months later she revealed that she had been watching the tape about five times a week. When I suggested that by now she must be bored to tears with it she exclaimed, "Oh no, I love it better each time. I get such joy looking at you, seeing you in your nice dress, hearing you talk so intelligent!" My mother was *kvelling* over me. I, in turn, felt enhanced.

We must realize that the mother who cannot *kvell* over her daughter may be neither malicious nor uncaring. Rather, she may suffer from low self-esteem and see her own short-comings in the daughter with whom she identifies. I am reminded of Enid who, as a child, had suffered teasing and other abuses from her classmates because she was fat. When Enid married and had a daughter, she became obsessed with the girl's weight. Although young Debbie was not model-skinny, neither was she overweight. Yet Enid made her feel increasingly self-conscious about her body. Watching her primp for a first date, Enid blurted out to thirteen-year-old Debbie, "You could be a pretty girl, you know, if you took off some pounds!" As soon as these words came out of her mouth, Enid felt ashamed. She knew that she was making it impossible for Debbie to feel attractive.

I recall, as well, an incident that my client Fern shared. When Fern, who is a lesbian, visited her mother, she was told by her, "It makes me uneasy to think that you are *that way*. I'd like it so much that when we're together you just don't mention your girlfriend. For the time you're with me, you can act *normal*." Fern explained that her mother believes that being gay is a sin and that, as a parent, she is responsible for her daughter's sexual orientation. In order to assuage her guilty feelings, she pretends that her daughter is heterosexual. Unfortunately, this solution ensures that Fern cannot be appreciated as she really is.

A story my grandmother once shared is particularly sad. Growing up in Vienna at the turn of the century, she desperately wanted to become a physician. However, because she was a woman, she was turned away from medical school.

It was her dream to have a son, who would not be held back as she was. After she gave birth to her third daughter, she refused to see the little girl for several days. When she finally took the baby from the nurse, she felt only anger and disappointment. "I wanted to bring a Peter into the world, a boy who would be strong and powerful, and all I could produce was a little Trudy, who would be a woman like me." It was not because of malice or natural coldness but rather because of her own feelings of inferiority that my grandmother could not look with shining, happy eyes upon her beautiful baby girl.

When children sense that their mother suffers from low self-esteem, they may suppress their own needs for recognition and approval and devote themselves to bolstering her self-image and to meeting her needs: They may become her sparkling mirror. In her book *The Drama of the Gifted Child*, psychoanalyst Alice Miller draws on a story by Alphonse Daudet that illustrates the tragedy of such a child.

Once upon a time there was a child who had a golden brain. His parents only discovered this by chance when he injured his head and gold instead of blood flowed out. They then began to look after him carefully and would not let him play with other children for fear of being robbed. When the boy was grown up and wanted to go out into the world, his mother said: "We have done so much for you, we ought to be able to share your wealth." Then her son took a large piece of gold out of his brain and gave it to his mother . . .[10]

As the story goes on, the young man continues to enhance others by giving up what is his. Weakened, impoverished, unhappy, his brain emptied out, he finally dies.

The mother who requires that her child mirror her, rather than the other way around, is a woman who herself has been robbed of vitality. She is wounded and in need of healing. Her young daughter, who loves her better than her own life, wants simply to make her well. But because she is small, relatively helpless and powerless, the little daughter—hard as she tries—cannot fix mother's life.

When I was small, I often saw fear and anxiety in my young mother's soft blue eyes. Both my parents had suffered persecution and unspeakable loss at Hitler's hands. The Nazis took their possessions, their jobs, their names (all Jews were renamed Israel or Sarah), and were responsible for the deaths of several of their relatives and their unborn child—the brother I would never know. With no financial resources, few marketable skills, and my father's elderly, infirm parents to support, my parents made their way to America in 1940. Four years later I was born into their lives, unplanned.

My mother once told me that when I was a baby, I would spit back at her the food she offered, but that as I got a little older I stopped being difficult and became a very good child. I do not remember being contrary, although during therapy I came to understand that rejecting my mother's food had been my way of rejecting the fear and anxiety she fed me. Thinking back, I remember only wanting to make her happy and to spare her from unnecessary upset or worry. Now I understand that because I thought my own fears would make my mother cry, I learned as a child to keep them hidden.

Although my parents, especially my stoical father, hardly spoke about the war years (no doubt to spare me), the horrors of their past infected my life, became indelibly etched in the very tissues of my body. I do not recall the exact age, but I remember that for a long period during childhood, when it was time to sleep, I dared not lay my head down and close my eyes. Like a soldier on watch, I sat up in bed propped against pillows, vigilantly keeping an eye on the fire escape outside my window so that when the Gestapo in black boots came for me in our New York City apartment, just as they had come for my father years before in Vienna,

I would be ready. At another time when I was a child I waited from day to day to be arrested and taken to jail because, during a pillow fight with my cousin, I had inadvertently pulled off from my pillow a tag that read: "THIS TAG IS NOT TO BE REMOVED UNDER PENALTY OF LAW." Because my father, who never did anything wrong, had been jailed and tortured just for being Jewish, I awaited harsh punishment for breaking a real law—pulling off a pillow tag. In school, I remember being always afraid—afraid of being called on and not knowing the answer, afraid of forgetting to do an assignment, afraid of talking when I shouldn't, afraid of asking for anything. Until I was in the fifth grade, I dared not ask to be excused to go to the bathroom.

In the end, although I tried, I failed to be the perfect little girl who was strong and brave and who, not being a trouble to anyone, made her mother always happy; I did not eat, suffered stomachaches, and developed a vivid hypochondria. Because my sickliness caused my mother much worry, I thought I was a bad and thankless child.

Psychiatrist E. James Anthony explains that mother and child live in a "hall of mirrors" that allows each to see one's self in the other. I can understand now that when my mother looked at me, her fear and anxiety must have deepened. Knowing what she knew, having lost what she lost, how could she believe that the infant girl with dark Jewish eyes whom she held in her arms could be safe, even in America? Reflected in her frightened eyes, I too became afraid—for her, for me. At forty-five, I am still struggling to contain some of these old fears.

Several months after the notorious *Kristall Nacht*, the night of shattered glass when the Nazi mobs vandalized the shops of Jewish merchants, my mother, newly wed and forcibly separated from her young husband (my father), fled Vienna by train. Not by choice, she traveled light—with only the clothes on her back—to begin a new life. Although my mother did not know, the baggage she was forced to leave behind encumbered me throughout my childhood and early adult years. Yet I learned in a dream that by opening the trunks and suitcases and examining their contents I could make them lighter as I proceeded on my journey.

# CHAPTER 2

# *Mothers as Role Models*

So boasting of her capacity to surround and protect, there was scarcely a shell left for her to know
herself by, all was so lavished and spent.

—Virginia Woolf
*To the Lighthouse*

Let me not forget that I am the daughter of a
woman who bent her head, trembling, between
the blades of a cactus, her wrinkled face full of
ecstacy over the promise of a flower, a woman
who herself never ceased to flower, untiringly during three quarters of a century.

—Colette
*Earthly Paradise*

Through a newborn's unsteady eyesight, the world
appears a blur; she cannot bring into focus objects that are
too near or too far. But from the vantage of mother's holding
arms, she is able to focus on mother's face, which is the
perfect distance from her own, and to see it with absolute
clarity. From this first moment of contact, she will never
again take her eyes off mother. Like the devoted scientist
who spends a lifetime studying the natural world, all daughters observe their mothers with passionate, sustained interest, and what they see profoundly affects who these
daughters become. The most fortunate among us discover
that mother is more than a mirror who nonjudgmentally
reflects what we assert; she is also a vital person in her own
right—a woman with a mind, talents, and ambitions of her
own.

In *Back Through the Glass*, a play written by my husband, Bruce Bassoff, four women and their adolescent daughters spend a weekend in a mountain cabin. On the first evening, one of the daughters suggests that they play a mother-daughter version of the "Newlywed Game." Each daughter is asked three personal questions about her mother, but before she answers, her mother privately writes down her own responses; the pair get a point every time their answers agree.

When Laura is asked, "If your mother had a wish, what would she wish for?" she answers, "I guess she'd wish for happiness for my brother and me."[1] With a twinkle in her eye, Jennifer, who is the most vivacious of the mothers, contradicts her daughter: "I'm more selfish than you think, I'd like to go to China,"[2] and, from Laura's wide smile, we know that she delights in her mother's "selfishness." Because Jennifer insists on an existence separate from that of her children and is able to assert her desires—her *self*-ness (a much better word than selfishness)—Laura need not feel guilty about claiming her own life; and she can believe that a positive mother-daughter bond does not require mutual self-sacrifice.

At the moment that Jennifer tells Laura that her biggest wish is to go to China, Ginger, one of the other mothers puffs herself up and whispers to her daughter, "Aren't you glad you've got the mother you've got, honey? My answer would have been your happiness."[3] At every performance of *Back Through the Glass*, this remark elicited groans from the audience. The mother who sacrifices her life for her children and then induces their guilt has become an object of derision—and laughter. "How many sons and daughters does it take to change Mom's light bulb?" the joke-teller asks, and then in a mock-whiny voice gives us the punch line, "None, because she'd rather sit in the dark."

Yet when I am counseling the daughters of self-sacrificing mothers, I usually find their stories to be sad instead of funny. For them, it is no joke that their mothers, because they have given up interests, talents, and ambitions, are devitalized and depressed. In fact, the poverty of their mothers' lives often triggers feelings of anger. As one client confides,

> When I picture my fifty-seven-year-old mother, I see her lying on the couch with a soaking compress on her head. I don't ask her to go places with me. I don't even talk to her about my comings and goings. She lets me know that everything is too much for her. She's a devoted mother, so maybe I shouldn't hate her for being a wet blanket. But I'm afraid I do.

More often than not, however, the adult daughter masks her anger because she is unsure of its legitimacy ("How can I rationalize my rage at a woman who has given up her life trying to make *me* happy?") or because she is wary of its destructive potential ("If I ever let my mother know how I hate her life, I would destroy her."). Underlying this anger are fear ("I am afraid that my life ultimately will be a copy of my mother's; *I am afraid that I will become my mother.*") and guilt ("I dare not have more than my mother has.").

We adult daughters feel most free to take for ourselves what our mothers took for themselves. We feel natural and comfortable experiencing what our mothers experienced. On the contrary, if our mothers deny (or are denied) their full lives and consequently know few pleasures, we are likely to restrict ourselves from living our own full lives. Although it makes no logical sense, by enjoying ourselves and becoming successful, we may somehow feel that we are taking what rightly belongs to our mothers; we feel guilty for having what they did not have. The following examples from my practice and my personal life illuminate how the mother who has not—by choice or circumstance—lived her own life fully may indirectly deprive her daughter.

Over pastries and a cup of tea, a womanfriend tells me how her mother's failure to have a loving relationship with a man influences her.

My mother's two marriages were stale, loveless. She warned me not to expect much from life and certainly not to expect anything from men. I hated her pessimism, especially her diatribes against men. As a young woman, I daydreamed, listened to romantic music on my portable radio, promised myself that my husband-to-be would be wonderful and that I would know true love. But now, to my horror, I am beginning to think like my mother: to expect nothing good from men. I have no idea how to love a man and to be loved by him. I'm beginning to understand that because she didn't believe she deserved true love, I am not allowing it either. This whole part of living—love and marriage—feels out of my reach.

A middle-aged client who has returned to college to complete a bachelor's degree becomes immobilized at finals time. Although she has done well up to this point, she cannot bring herself to study. She knows she is sabotaging herself but feels unable to pull herself out of the hole into which she is sinking. In our sessions, she tells me about her mother.

My mother dropped out of high school to marry and have kids. She doesn't have a life outside the home. I have never seen her pick up a book to read, and when my brothers and father have discussions about current events, she walks out of the room.

My client fears that she will not succeed as a student because her mother gave up all intellectual pursuits: "I am powerless against her. Something inside me stops me from going beyond her."

During a therapy session, a college student, living away from home for the first time, describes her reclusive mother as suspicious of everyone outside the family. Although the young woman wants to be tolerant of her own friends, she admits being hypercritical of them. After phone conversations with her mother, she becomes especially irritable: "It's awful, but for days after I've spoken to Mom, I am so fault-finding that my roommates don't want to be around me." I suggest that by assuming her mother's unattractive characteristics, she is creating an illusion of mother-daughter oneness; in sharing her mother's dim view of people, she becomes closer to her. Agreeing with my interpretation, my young client adds, "And when I'm open to the world around me—so different from the way she is—I feel somehow that I'm showing her up."

Another client maintains loyalty to her mother in a similar way. To an outsider, this young woman appears as self-assured and accomplished as any of the new-age women who shine on the glossy pages of *Working Woman* magazine. A feminist, she is an outspoken critic of the ways her father held her mother back from making a career. Yet—subconsciously mimicking her mother's lifestyle—she herself chooses to remain in a love relationship with a man who does not support her independence. Always at his beck and call, she will put off her own work as a writer in order to run errands for him. "I don't act myself with him. But, oddly enough, sometimes I feel comfortable pretending to be very domestic, very traditional, very nonassertive—just like Mom. At other times, I am in a rage with him because when we are together I turn into this submissive person whom *I* don't like."

I am with a womanfriend in a fine restaurant. The waiter sets splendid dishes, which are quite costly, before us. My friend smiles and assures me that we deserve this luxury every once in a while, but suddenly I feel nauseated. I begin to think about my parents and the plain way we lived when I was small. In my mind's eye, I see my mother coming home dead on her feet from her sales job in the family-run bakery; I see her washing out her white nylon uniform in the bathtub, putting up supper, doing the dishes. I see my father, tired after his long hours in the hot bakery, pasting

Green Stamps at the kitchen table and hear him telling me how we will redeem them one day for "luxuries" like a stepping stool or a new saucepan; I see him shopping for groceries, examining every can of fruit cocktail on the shelf in an effort to find the one mismarked at a lower price. I am at once warmed and suffocated by the modesty of their lives. For an instant, I imagine my parents sitting in this plush restaurant with me, but the image is painful because they look so out of place. Now I feel very sick to my stomach: "What am I doing here?" I ask myself.

To a large extent, our mothers' lives are models for our own. If our mothers are able to love and to be loved, we tend to expect good relationships; if our mothers were successful in school, we are likely to be confident of our intellectual capacities; if our mothers are friendly, we are probably easy around people; if our mothers were independent, we generally take pride in our autonomy; if our mothers indulge in the good life, we tend to feel comfortable shopping in better stores or dining in fine restaurants. On the contrary, if our mothers lead restricted lives, we may find it difficult to take advantage of the chances to be happy and successful.

As a young girl I heard a story that underscores the difference between the opportunities that life holds and what we dare allow ourselves.

Once upon a time there was a poor old man who suffered undeserved abuse at the hands of his neighbors. When he died and went to Heaven, the angels at Heaven's Gate were eager to compensate him for the pleasures he had missed on earth. "Dear man," they chimed, "we are ready to reward you for the humble and good life you have led. You knew so little happiness in your lifetime, yet you never complained. Be assured that here in Heaven you may have anything you wish. Please, tell us what you want." The good man was stunned by the angels' generosity, but unused to kindness, could not bring himself to make a request. Finally, after much coaxing from them, he stammered, "If it is not too much to ask, I would like a fresh roll to eat." Taken aback by his modesty, the angels gently urged him to indulge his fancies, "Dear man, be more bold, for here in Heaven you can have *anything* your heart desires." After much deliberation he inquired, "Might I then have my roll buttered?"

The humble man in this tale reminds me of the daughter of the woman with a small life. Although the world, like the angels, may offer her wonderful possibilities, she is reluctant to claim them. Because her mother's life is spare, she does not know that hers can be rich; because her mother was deprived, she does not believe she deserves to be full.

Very often, the mother who lives a restricted life is merely living out the self-denying, self-sacrificing role society assigned her. When, in the 1970s, Marlo Thomas produced her wonderful album, *Free to be . . . you and me*,[4] she stunned me (then a full-time mother of a newborn and a toddler) with the revolutionary idea that women—women with children—could be mothers *and* at the same time people with interesting careers and interesting minds. Embarrassed as I am to admit this to my feminist friends, I had not previously entertained the possibilities she presented.

Sometimes I forget that when my own mother was raising me, Marlo Thomas's liberating songs did not exist. My mother did not know that she might strive for more than she had. I remember a time when as a young woman I took my mother to an art museum, a place we would not ordinarily go to together. We came to Degas's studies of the laundry women—portraits of women with vacant faces and tired bodies, who are pressing clothes and carrying heavy baskets of laundry. My mother stood in front of these paintings for a long time, then whispered, "I like these very much. I know how the women are feeling." I wanted to put my arms around her, but I knew that if I did, I would not be

able to hold back my tears. Without knowing, she was breaking my heart.

When I was gathering material for this chapter, I came
across a plethora of literature written in the first half of this
century that instructed women to give up their talents and
ambitions on behalf of their families. The wise woman, the
literature made clear, is "forgetful of self" and committed to
an "unselfish life of sacrifice and devotion." As a conversation between Norine and Priss, characters in Mary Mc-
Carthy's 1950s novel *The Group*, demonstrates, even
intellectual development was a forbidden pleasure.

> "Our Vassar education made it tough for me to accept
> my womanly role. . . . The trouble is my brains. . . ." Priss
> was surprised. . . . Brains, she thought to herself were
> supposed to help you organize your life efficient-
> ly. . . .
> "You really feel your education was a mistake?" Priss
> asked anxiously.
> "Oh, completely," said Norine. "I've been crippled for
> life."[5]

Although we may shake our heads in disbelief at the Norines
of past generations, many of us are not yet free of the self-
denigrating attitudes that defined our mothers' lives. And
even when we disapprove of the ways they lived, we can
easily fall into the same patterns.

New research in the field of infant development is providing scientific evidence for what many daughters know
intuitively: Watching our mothers, we absorb their beliefs;
reading their faces, we often learn what is (and is not) possible for us. In the "visual cliff" experiments conducted by
Doctors Mary Klinnert, Joseph Campos, and Robert Emde,[6]
an infant is placed at the edge of a glass table. Special lighting
effects make the glass surface appear invisible and the red-
and-white checkered cloth, which is directly beneath the
glass, look like solid ground. The baby's mother stands at
the opposite end of the glass table next to a bright and

beautiful toy ferris wheel. Excitedly, the baby crawls toward mother and the ferris wheel, but when she reaches the half-way point, she notices that the checkered cloth below her no longer seems to be solid ground. The experimenters have designed the cloth so that it appears to drop precipitously; the baby has the illusion of being at the edge of a high cliff. When she looks down, she is naturally scared and is tempted to stop her journey to return to safe ground; at the same time, she wants to get to mother and the pretty toy. Unable to resolve her ambivalence, the child looks toward her mother to assess her emotional response to the situation. If mother has been instructed to show fear on her face, baby does not cross the imaginary cliff. But if mother is smiling and confident, baby masters the "cliff" and crawls toward her.

The experimenters call this behavior "social referencing": When the baby is in doubt she refers to mother's affect— the expression that conveys the message "Come on, darling, you're doing fine" or "Go back, it's too dangerous out there." My clinical work with adult daughters and my life experiences convince me that as we determine which paths to follow, we continue to refer to mother for recognition and encouragement; more than a mirror that reflects what we assert, mother is often a crystal ball that suggests what we can expect from the world. If she is strong and resolute she waves us on, but if she is self-denying, self-sacrificing, and insecure she can hold us back.

A client, Elise, recounts her mother's influence on her life.

When, shortly after I married, I told my mother that my husband had hit me a couple of times and that I was mustering up the courage to leave him, she hugged me and told me to put up with the "unpleasantness," just as she had put up with my alcoholic father's abuse for thirty-two years. Months after my divorce, I still feel pangs of guilt. In my head I know that I did the right thing to leave my brutish husband, but in my heart I feel I was wrong to think of myself first. I'm still calling him all the time, taking care of him, just as I did when we were married.

I remember that when I was applying to graduate school, my mother, in her most fearful voice, asked, "But do you have a right to go back to school? Has Bruce given you permission? What will it do to your marriage if you get a Ph.D?" I remember becoming angry at her, telling her that I did not need my husband's *permission* to make a life for myself—this was after I had listened to Marlo Thomas's songs!—but I also remember that my mother's concern made me anxious and that during the years I balanced graduate work with family life, I half-believed that I was doing something wrong, that I was being selfish, and that maybe I would lose my husband.

Even in this age of the modern, liberated woman, it remains difficult for many of us to pursue the education or careers or creative work or love relationships or joie de vivre that our mothers deny themselves. Virginia Woolf understood this all too well when she presented her scathing indictment of the Good Mother.

> I will describe her as shortly as I can. She was intensely sympathetic. She was immensely charming. She was utterly unselfish. She excelled in the difficult arts of family life. She sacrificed herself daily. . . . She was constituted that she never had a mind or a wish of her own, but preferred to sympathize always with the minds and wishes of other[s]. . . .
>
> I now record the one act for which I take some credit to myself. . . . I turned upon her and caught her by the throat. I did my best to kill her. My excuse, if I were to be had up in a court of law, would be that I acted in self-defence. Had I not killed her she would have killed me. She would have plucked the heart out of my writing. . . . Thus whenever I felt the shadow of her wing or the radiance of her halo upon my page I took up the inkpot and flung it at her. It is far harder to kill a phantom than a reality. She

was always creeping back when I thought I had dispatched her. Though I flatter myself that I killed her in the end, the struggle was severe; it took much time that had better have been spent upon learning Greek grammar or roaming the world in search of adventures.[7]

Woolf is correct to insist that we free ourselves from the angel mother's grip. Yet *killing* her is a desperate and unsatisfactory solution. Indeed, Woolf's suicide can be understood partially as a consequence of her unresolved filial anger and suggests that if we are to lead unfettered, fully realized lives, we must eventually find better solutions for our troubled relationships than simply raging at them. (I deal with such solutions in the second part of this book.) Nevertheless, Woolf deserves much credit. At a time in our history when it was popular to idealize self-denial and self-sacrifice, she accurately saw how the Angel of the House, the proverbial Good Mother, debilitates her child.

The daughter of the deprived, self-less woman is not only likely to hold herself back from living life fully but, in extreme circumstances, she may devote herself to enhancing her mother. Observing mother with ever-watchful eyes, many young daughters discover that they can soothe her. They may learn, for example, that when they are attentive to mother or sweet and buoyant, they can cheer her up; but when they are worried or depressed they aggravate her despair. Or they may learn quite the opposite: Becoming depressed *with* mother helps her feel warm and loved but failing to join in her sadness or anxiety promotes her loneliness. Eventually these supremely dutiful daughters screen out behaviors that threaten mother's comfort and assume only those that please her. Although they may at first enjoy their status as mother's special girls ("the jewel in my mother's crown,"[8] as one of Alice Miller's psychiatric patients described herself), as time goes on, they will understand that it has cost them too much. The following passage, by novelist and short story writer Alice Munro, touchingly reveals the burden borne by one such special girl.

> I went around the house to the back door, thinking, I have
> been to a dance and a boy has walked me home and kissed
> me. It was all true. My life was possible. I went past the
> kitchen window and I saw my mother. She was sitting
> with her feet on the open oven door, drinking tea out of
> a cup without a saucer. She was just sitting and waiting
> for me to come home and tell her everything that had
> happened. And I would not do it, I never would. But when
> I saw the waiting kitchen, and my mother in her faded,
> fuzzy Paisley kimono, with her sleepy but doggedly expectant face, I understood what a mysterious and oppressive obligation I had, to be happy, and how I had almost
> failed it, and would be likely to fail it, every time, and she
> would not know.[9]

The Yiddish word *nachas* refers to the heightened status and personal enhancement a parent receives as a result of her child's achievements ("My wonderful daughter has given me three beautiful grandchildren. What *nachas* she brings me!"). *Nachas* is different from *kvelling*, which describes the joy experienced not at what the child *does* for the parent but rather for who the child *is*. Sadly, some daughters, believing that their mothers are poor in talent, opportunities, accomplishment, or joy, feel their most important purpose in life is "to bring Mama lots of *nachas*"—to be the jewel in her plain crown. They do not believe that they have value apart from meeting mother's needs.

In extreme cases, they may begin to experience themselves not as an "I" but as an "it." Like a commodity—a car or a washing machine, for example—whose value is determined by its serviceability, they feel worthwhile only if they are serving mother (or others, such as husband or children or employer, who later take mother's place) by making her happy or proud. The following case study, drawn from my practice, is an example of this kind of debilitating attachment.

Twenty-six-year-old April first came to see me because she suffered from high levels of anxiety. The increasing recognition she was getting at work for her excellent administrative skills seemed to trigger this anxiety, which she experienced as a forbidding presence looming over her. After her supervisor rewarded her with a promotion and a hefty raise in salary, April had her worst attack: "When my boss said that he was giving me a raise, I felt so pleased with myself. But soon after, I began to get anxious. I started fantasizing that a burglar would break into my apartment and take all my nice things. Later, things got even worse because I was convinced that someone wanted to murder me."

In order to understand the meaning of April's anxiety, I needed to know more about her background. As she explained, her childhood had been a friendless one. Because her father was restless and unsatisfied, he had moved his family from one city to another, so that they never settled in a place long enough to become part of a community. A distant and inaccessible man, April's father was not affectionate with his children or with his wife. Without a doubt, April's most important relationship was with her mother, Lydia, an emotionally frail woman, who suffered terribly from loneliness. Separated from her own parents and sisters, on whom she had relied before her marriage, she turned to April, her oldest child, for companionship.

Flashing back on her early years, April pictured herself sitting close to mother on their plaid Castro convertible as, hour after hour, they watched game shows on TV. To be sure, as April pointed out, her mother amply praised her for being so attentive: "April," she would often say, "whatever would I do without you? You're the light of my life. I'm so lonely when we're not together." However, out of her great need for her daughter's constant companionship,

Lydia held her back from developing warm relationships with others: "Now, remember April, come home right after school. It's our afternoon to bake bread," or, "Something about the little girl who lives next door bothers me, so I don't want you playing with her," or "That French teacher you like so much has all the wrong ideas about education; I wouldn't trust her if I were you."

Despite her over-attachment to Lydia, April did muster the courage to leave home to attend college out of state. However, while at school, she fell into a suicidal depression: "I felt so awful for abandoning my mother that I suppose I thought I should be punished for this by dying." Although April was resistant to the idea, I suggested that her fantasies of suicide were also a way of punishing her mother, that is, a disguised way of saying, "I am prepared to do violence to myself to demonstrate my terrible anger against you. I am ready to annihilate your 'special little girl' just as you have annihilated me."

After graduating from college, April settled into her own apartment and found a promising job. But despite the outward signs of having separated from mother, April still struggled to justify an independent existence, and she was still depressed. As she once told me,

Crazy as this seems, I feel *illegal* for having my life. I think I have to prove somehow that I deserve to be alive. I do this by being very careful to please others, never making anyone mad at me. But, even when I'm on my best behavior, *I know* that I don't deserve a life. I then worry that sooner or later other people will find out what is so clear to me.

April and I came to understand that having relinquished the role of mother's all-fulfilling daughter, she was at a loss. As mother's special girl, April had some status; as her own person, she had none—or so she thought. Moreover, because Lydia valued April more as an extension of herself— her comforter, confidante, and companion—rather than a person in her own right, April never really learned to value her *self*.

Let us now return to April's presenting problem—her work-related anxieties. As we discovered during our therapy sessions, these too were at least in part related to her relationship with mother. Although Lydia was in one way an affectionate, involved mother, April, who over many years watched her so intently, saw a hidden side: Lydia was also a hostile woman who seemed to take secret pleasure in ridicule and scorn. As I pointed out to April, *every person who cannot engage her own life fully envies people blessed with vitality.* (How could she not?) What had been painful but necessary for April to understand was that Lydia not only envied people outside the family circle—April's teachers, potential friends, and romantic interests, for example—she also envied her special daughter.

The Grimm Brothers' fairy tale "Snow White and the Seven Dwarfs" provides perhaps the best-known example of maternal envy. Whereas the enhancing mother takes vicarious pleasure in her child's blossoming, Snow White's envious stepmother, the Queen, fails to identify with her in a positive way. Peering into her looking glass to ask who is the fairest in the land, she becomes increasingly furious when, instead of her own image, that of her pretty stepdaughter appears. Determined to destroy the girl, she orders her huntsman to kill Snow White and to return with her lungs and liver as evidence. When the soft-hearted huntsman returns from his gruesome assignment with the lungs and liver of an animal, the Queen, believing they are the innards of Snow White, has them cooked in salt and then eats them. Just as primitive man and woman believed they could acquire the characteristics or powers of what they ate, the Queen tries to incorporate Snow White's beauty and sexuality by consuming her internal organs.

Lydia, too, fed off her daughter, whose happiness she wanted—for herself. Unable to empathize or join with April's natural exuberance, as healthy mothers can, Lydia rather *sucked it in* to fill up her own empty, aching, hungry soul.

April recalled, for example, that in being with her mother, she usually felt depleted.

> At school I was energetic, full of enthusiasm, but as soon as I came home to mother, I would feel an enormous tiredness take me over. I'd look at Mom's longing face and know she wanted something more from me—always more.

Because her own mother envied and exploited her, April fantasized that others would also want and take what she had: A burglar would steal her most treasured possessions; a murderer would kill her as punishment for her raise and promotion. To protect herself against others' imagined envy, April hid her achievements and talents from their view. Her supervisor's persistence in recognizing her, however, cracked her protective shell and thereby precipitated her paranoia about lurking burglars and murderers, which led her to undertake therapy. In order to heal—as she eventually did—April had to relinquish the role of all-fulfilling daughter, and she had to accept the legitimacy, safety, and "rightness" of a life separate from and more rewarding than her mother's.

In my daily practice as psychologist, I do not usually hear of mothers as empty and needy as Lydia. I do, however, regularly encounter daughters as devoted as April had been. For the whole of our lives, we daughters tend to remain intensely loyal and committed to our mothers, and, sadly, some of us are ready to sacrifice all in order to make her whole and happy. As one of Miller's wounded patients dreamed: "I see a green meadow, on which there is a white coffin. I am afraid that my mother is in it, but I open up the lid, and, luckily, it is not my mother but me."[10]

The most enhancing mother, we are learning, is not the woman who gives up her life. Rather she is the woman who lives it fully and, by virtue of this fact, encourages her child to do the same. Of all the tributes to mothers that I have read, those of the French writer Colette—whom literary critic Louise Bernikow calls "the poet of passion between mother and daughter"—are most memorable.[11] Not surprisingly, Colette does not pay homage to a self-sacrificing, self-abnegating mother but describes instead, with loving admiration, a woman who until her dying day enjoyed life passionately.

> It was not until one morning when I found the kitchen unwarmed and the blue enamel saucepan hanging on the wall, that I felt my mother's end to be near. Her illness knew many respites, during which the fire flared up again on the hearth, and the smell of fresh bread and melting chocolate stole under the door together with the cat's impatient paw. These respites were periods of unexpected alarms. My mother and the big walnut cupboard were discovered together in a heap at the foot of the stairs, she having determined to transport it in secret from the upper landing to the ground floor. Whereupon my elder brother insisted that my mother should keep still and that an old servant should sleep in the little house. But how could an old servant prevail against a vital energy so youthful and mischievous that it contrived to tempt and lead astray a body already half fettered by death? My brother, returning before sunrise from attending a distant patient, one day caught my mother red-handed in the most wanton of crimes. Dressed in her nightgown, but wearing heavy gardening sabots, her little grey septuagenarian's plait of hair turning up like a scorpion's tail on the nape of her neck, one foot firmly planted on the beech trestle, her back bent in the attitude of the expert jobber, my mother, rejuvenated by an indescribable expression of guilty enjoyment, in defiance of all her promises and of the freezing morning dew, was sawing logs in her own yard.[12]

Having internalized her mother's vitality, Colette never allowed her own enjoyment of life to slacken. Two days before his wife's death, Colette's husband wrote,

She pointed to the boxes of butterflies on their shelf, the book, and the birds in the garden. "Ah," she said. So near to death and knowing it, everything appeared to her more beautiful and more wonderful than ever. Her hands fluttered about her like wings. She leaned a bit closer to me. Her arm described a spiral which embraced everything that she had shown me: "Look!" she said to me. "Maurice, look!"[13]

Shortly before his own death, another writer, Joseph Campbell, who had spent a lifetime studying mythology and religion, was asked what his scholarly work had taught him, and he answered, to "follow your bliss." The mother who relishes and celebrates her own precious life allows her daughter to follow her bliss. Those of us daughters who as children had fulfilled mothers are fortunate indeed. But those of us who did not are sometimes able to encourage our mothers, no matter what their age, to take new pleasure and have adventures now—for their sake and for ours too.

When I was a little girl, my parents and I spent summers in a resort in the Catskill Mountains, where my father worked as a baker. For the evening's entertainment, the guests and staff would often gather around a piano and sing or simply laugh and joke among themselves. Because I was a small child, I was always put to bed before the fun began. One night, however, I sneaked out of my room and made my way to the main hall. Crouching unseen behind an overstuffed chair, I caught sight of my parents waltzing as the guests stood around and applauded them. With her golden hair and blue eyes shimmering, my mother looked like a beautiful fairy-tale princess; and my father, tall and handsome, was her prince. My eyes fixed on this magical scene for a long time, and then my father noticed me. The spell was broken. I was gently admonished and sent back to my room.

Yet, when I am happiest, I sometimes draw on this memory. The image of my young, fun-loving parents dipping and swirling to Strauss's Viennese music reminds me that, although I sometimes suffer from bouts of anxiety and depression, I follow in their footsteps and am also able to dance with joy. And the image of my mother's face—at that moment radiant without a trace of sadness or fear—reminds me that just as she was the mother who sometimes wounded, she was also the mother who blessed.

# CHAPTER 3

# Missing Mothercare: The Unprotected Daughter

Backward, turn backward, O Time, in your flight,
Make me a child again, just for to-night!
Mother, come back from the echoless shore,
Take me again to your heart, as of yore;
Kiss from my forehead the furrows of care,
Smooth the few silver threads out of my hair,
Over my slumbers your loving watch keep,—
Rock me to sleep, mother, rock me to sleep!
                              —Elizabeth Akers Allen
                              "Rock Me to Sleep, Mother"


Rabbi Hillel's familiar saying, "If I am not for my-self, who will be for me? But if I am only for myself, what am I?"[1] reminds us that humane living requires a balance. The enhancing mother learns—and what a challenge it is!—to take precious care of her own life *and* to protect and nurture the lives of her dependent children.[2] In the previous chapter we looked at the ways daughters are adversely affected by self-sacrificing mothers. In this chapter we will look at the ways we are affected by under-protective mothers, both during childhood and long after. In addition to exploring the consequences of too little care, we will also explore the nature of appropriate maternal protection and nurturance; for if, as children, we did not have the comfort and security of mothercare, we need to know now what exactly we missed so that we can both mourn and compensate for our early loss.

*        *        *

Of the many newspaper stories of suffering and courage
that emerged from the tragedy of the 1988 Armenian earth-
quake, one in particular haunts and touches me. On that
cold December day, four-year-old Gayaney and her mother,
Susanna Petrosyan, were visiting with the child's aunt, Karine, who lived in an apartment building in the small city of
Leninkan. While Gayaney watched, Susanna tried on some
clothes that Karine was selling. She had just slipped out of
an especially pretty black party dress with puffed sleeves
when the furniture began to tremble, then to shake violently.
Dressed only in her undergarments, Susanna grabbed Gayaney and ran to the door, but before they could reach safety
the floor opened up and the walls around them collapsed.

Susanna, Gayaney, and Karine fell into the cellar, trapped
by tons of smashed concrete and debris. Pinned on her back,
Susanna discovered that she could nevertheless move
slightly from side to side. Groping among the rubble in the
bitter-cold darkness, she discovered a jar of blackberry jam
as well as a piece of cloth, which she folded and slid under
her daughter to make a little bed. Although Susanna was
very cold, she pulled off her stockings and wrapped them
around Gayaney's head to keep her warm. On the second
day of their entrapment—the day Karine died of her inju-
ries—Susanna gave the entire contents of the jar of blackberry jam to her hungry child. As the days and nights of
brutal cold and total darkness passed, Gayaney no longer
asked for food, but her pleas for something to drink became
increasingly pressing: "Mommy, I need a drink. Please,
Mommy, give me something." Susanna hallucinated and
saw bottles of lemonade, but when she reached out to touch
them, they disappeared. Without water or fruit juice or other
liquid, Susanna thought that her little daughter would soon
die of thirst. Desperate to save the child's life, Susanna cut
open her fingers with a shard of glass and, with her own
blood, nursed the little girl. On the eighth day of their cap-

tivity, rescue workers—Susanna's husband among them—discovered Gayaney and Susanna and rushed them to the hospital.

Asked to explain how the two survived their ordeal, Susanna's doctor suggested that the infusions of her mother's blood were probably not the critical factor for Gayaney: "What saved them was that they were together. The mother didn't have time to panic. She had to think of the child."[3]

After I read about the Petrosyans in my local paper, I clipped the article and tucked it away in a desk drawer. From time to time, I pull it out to look at the photograph of the dark-eyed, dark-haired Gayaney propped up by pillows in her hospital bed; the smiling eyes brim with trust. Although the walls around Gayaney collapsed, her mother did not cave in; instead she did what the good, protective mother should do: *she contained the young child's fears, anxieties, and psychological pain through a soothing maternal presence.*

In *The Uses of Enchantment*, child psychiatrist Bruno Bettelheim refers to a Turkish fairy tale about a boy named Iskender who is put into a casket and set adrift on the ocean. Iskender encounters many dangers, but a green bird comes to him each time he is threatened and says, "Know that you are never deserted."[4] Protective and soothing, Susanna Petrosyan is the green bird incarnate, who reminds her child that she is never deserted.


The good mother is one whose care of her child changes to accommodate the stages of the child's development. When, for example, we are very young, we require her faithful protection and abundant generosity. We need her not only to feed, shelter, and clothe us but also to soothe our baby bodies, which are exquisitively sensitive to the myriad internal and external stimuli that impinge upon them.[5] If mother consistently soothes us when we are overwhelmed by hunger, pain, fear, or anxiety, we learn that the world—which she represents—is basically good and that in it we are basically safe. If, instead, she consistently ignores or misinterprets our needs, we learn to mistrust the world and are afraid in it.

During the early months and years of life, those of us blessed with a protective and nurturing mother absorb her healing spirit so that it naturally becomes part of ourselves— an internalized, or inner, mother on whom we can later call to quell the emotional distress that life entails. When, for example, I come down with one of my incapacitating migraine headaches, which are my nemesis, I retreat to a darkened room to lie down; after a time I usually feel a cool, gentle hand resting on my forehead—and although she lives hundreds of miles away, I know the hand is my mother's.

Because most of us do not remember events from infancy, we cannot readily conjure images of our caretaking mothers. But in the collective art and literature of our civilization, we can rediscover her. Primitive cultures represented her as a vessel, which contains, protects, nourishes, and, like a cor- nucopia, is the giver of riches. The ancient Egyptians saw her as Nut, the goddess of heaven and sky, who protectively bends over the earth, enveloping all humankind under a cover of clouds and warmth. Other early cultures revered her as the principle of earth and nature: She is the flowing water and the milk of the sacred herds; the sheltering cave and mountain; the fruit-bearing tree; the abundance of veg- etative life in forests and steppe, mountains and valleys. In our fairy tales, she is the fourteen angels who watch over Hansel and Gretel as they sleep, and she is the little hazelnut tree that offers Cinderella solace.

In our modern literature, the protective and nurturing early mother is evoked through Colette's lush descriptions of her own childhood. Sido is the tender mother who carried the half-sleeping Colette, the "Little One," to her bed: "The two arms were so gentle, so careful to hold me close enough to protect my dangling feet at every doorway."[6] She is the mother who awakened Colette's senses and "smelled of laundered cretonne, of irons heated on the poplar-wood fire, of lemon-verbena leaves which she rolled between her palms or thrust into her pocket" and at nightfall of "newly watered lettuces."[7] And she is the mother of the hearth, "the centre and the secret birthplace whence radiate . . . the warm sitting room with its flora of cut branches and its fauna of peaceful creatures; the echoing house, dry, warm and crackling as a newly-baked loaf."[8] Because Colette experienced Sido as wonderfully protective not only of her own children but of all things that live and grow, her motherly spirit materializes as the image of an enclosed garden to which Colette can always return for rest and comfort. It is "a warm, confined enclosure reserved for the cultivation of aubergines and pimentos—where the smell of tomato leaves mingled in July with that of the apricots ripening."[9]

To be sure, Sido, as described by Colette, is idealized; she seems more goddess mother than human mother. But we must recognize that Sido is seen through the eyes of the young child Colette once was—and that every young child idealizes to one degree or another her protectress, on whom she depends absolutely.

When I was two, my maternal grandmother, who had been living in England, joined our household to take care of me so that my mother could return to work. Although with her own daughters—especially the youngest—she was at times under-protective, for me, my story-telling grandmother was a magical figure who, better than anyone else, dispelled my terrible fears. (It is not uncommon that less-than-adequate parents can become more-than-adequate grandparents.) Through her wonderful make-believe, she brought into my life a family of guardian angels and good fairies whose pillow fights made snowflakes, whose tears made rain, whose smiles made rainbows, and, most important, whose love and kindness made me feel safe.

In contrast to the world of Nazis in black boots waiting to ensnare me, which I had created out of my parents' wartime experiences, my grandmother's enchanted inventions instilled in me new feelings of well-being. With a family of winged celestial spirits watching over me, my fears about the world abated. My grandmother intuitively understood that a young child, who cannot yet care for herself, must believe that powerful, loving others—in my case, the guardian angels and good fairies she created for me—safeguard her. Until I was more capable to survive in the real world, I was served well by believing in their supernatural powers.

Less fortunate daughters may not have a protective maternal figure. When a mother is unsure of herself as a parent and as a woman or when she is too wrapped up in herself, she may abdicate her protective role prematurely. Waiting on line in a restaurant, I overheard a woman, in the presence of a girl who appeared to be five or six, tell a companion: "The doctor told me that my blood pressure is up and that I need to take better care of myself if I want to live!" At this, the child anxiously inquired, "Oh, Mommy, will you be okay?" and the woman impatiently replied, "I don't know. All I know is what the doctor said."

I could not get this scene out of my mind for days. The young child who is so vulnerable and dependent on her caretakers needs to believe in their strength and constancy; knowing that she cannot yet care for herself, she needs to know that they will be there for her. It was, I am quite sure, a mistake for this mother to speak so openly and so alarmingly about her health problem in the child's presence. Yet I know that being only human, parents do sometimes slip and say things that their children are not ready to hear. More disturbing to me is the woman's reply to the little girl's anxious question. A more protective mother would have offered reassurances. She might have said something like this: "I can understand that what you just overheard scares you. *But you don't have to worry about me.* The doctor told me what I need to do to stay healthy, and I will do everything he said." A protective mother does not deny reality—in this case, for example, that there is a health problem—but neither does she burden her child unnecessarily; moreover, a protective mother conveys the sense that when problems do arise, she can meet them with reasonable confidence.

Protecting one's children is not always easy or obvious. Only recently, our fifteen-year-old son told us that remarks made by some of his teachers and casual conversations between my husband and me about the "dismal state of the planet" alarmed him when he was young. Hearing that no one—not his teachers, not us, not even the president of the United States—could control the threats to the environment or the worldwide problems of war, disease, overpopulation, and famine, he became convinced that we were all doomed. Parents cannot shield their children from all harsh realities, but my husband and I are learning that we are appropriately protective when we convey to our son and daughter the message that situations are never hopeless, that problems have solutions, and that we are not helpless.

Unhappily, not all mothers are sufficiently nurturant or protective during the child's early years. We have many explanations for under-mothering. Some mothers nurture poorly because they do not understand what a small child needs in order to thrive. During a therapy session, for example, a teenage client began scolding her infant son for fussing and crying. Believing that the three-week-old child was purposely interfering with our conversation, she was quite surprised when I explained that little babies cry because they are hurting, not because they are being manipulative.

Some mothers who are very unsure of themselves may become overwhelmed by their child's normal demands; instead of calming the overwrought child, they make her even more anxious by their own anxiety. As one client remembers, "When I went to my mother with a childish problem, she inevitably overreacted, 'Oh, how terrible! What ever can we do?' so that I felt worse for talking to her. Consequently, I learned to keep my troubles to myself. Even now I am reluctant to get support because I don't want to upset anyone."

Some mothers suffer from a mental or physical illness that interferes with caretaking. In her memoir, political activist Gloria Steinem describes her mentally impaired mother who "lay in bed with eyes closed and lips moving in occasional response to voices only she could hear," and "tried hard to clean our littered house whenever she emerged from her private world, but who could rarely be counted on to finish one task." Reflecting what must be the terrible loss of every under-mothered child, she writes, "I miss her, but perhaps no more in death than I did in life."[10]

Some mothers who are poor and forced to work outside the home may not find adequate substitute caretakers for their small children. In her poignant short story "I Stand Here Ironing," Tillie Olsen describes the anguish of one such parent whose harsh circumstances prevent her from nurturing and protecting her daughter.

> She was a beautiful baby. She blew bubbles of sound. She loved motion, loved light, loved color and music and textures. . . . She was a miracle to me, but when she was eight months old I had to leave her daytimes with the woman downstairs to whom she was no miracle at all, for I worked or looked for work and for Emily's father, who "could no longer endure" (he wrote in his good-bye note) "sharing want with us."
>
> I was nineteen. It was pre-relief, pre-WPA world of the depression. I would start running as soon as I got off the streetcar, running up the stairs, the place smelling sour, and awake or asleep to startle awake, when she saw me she would break into a clogged weeping that could not be comforted, a weeping I can hear yet."[11]

And some mothers, because they were once victims of parental cruelty, heap abuse on their innocent children. Cruel words, humiliations, scorn, beatings, sexual violations are never really forgotten; they are absorbed into the body and the soul where they fester and are often later discharged in harmful ways. As one of my clients remarked:

> I understand now that my mother must have carried an enormous but silent rage against her own mother, who

used to beat her to a pulp for the slightest show of diso-
bedience. My mother took that rage and directed it against
me. How many wooden hangers did she break over my
poor back, I wonder.

Whatever the reasons for her failures, the mother who
does not consistently respond to the young daughter's needs
for food, shelter, warmth, and, just as important, *soothing*
promotes a basic mistrust: The world—represented by
mother—is expected to deprive, disappoint, frustrate, or
punish more often than not. Moreover, as the following case
study illustrates, the child who was not adequately protected
and nurtured may, as she grows up, fail to develop ways
of soothing herself when she is in distress; because she has
not been sufficiently mothered, she may not know how to
give herself loving care. For her there may not be a green
bird to whisper reassurances or an enclosing garden to provide solace.


Lillian, a woman in her early thirties, requested an appointment with me to deal with an impending transfer from
one branch of the corporation where she worked to another.
Because Lillian enjoyed her present placement, she was upset by the involuntary transfer; over the previous week, for
example, she had not gotten a full night's sleep, had little
appetite, and was often teary-eyed. At our first meeting, I
explained that the symptoms she presented were normal
depressive reactions to her imminent loss and that within
weeks they would most likely pass; in the meantime I suggested weekly supportive psychotherapy. That night, however, Lillian, in a state of great agitation, called me and
insisted that she could not bear her psychological discomfort.
Would I not refer her immediately for antidepressants or
tranquilizers? I wondered why Lillian was feeling so out-of-
control, why the threatened transfer was plunging her into
such a deep crisis. We scheduled an appointment for the
next morning.

During our session, I learned that Lillian did not know how to soothe—or *mother*—herself when she was distressed. In the past, if something had disturbed her, she would wash away her troubles by drinking a few glasses of wine or by raiding the refrigerator for goodies. But in her present situation these external solutions did not seem to work; and Lillian, "feeling unglued," was frantic.

As we talked, I discovered that Lillian's mother had generally been unable to soothe Lillian when she was small. For example, Lillian remembered that one time she came rushing into her mother's sewing room and, tears running down her face, held up the bruised little finger that she had just caught in a kitchen drawer. Impatiently, her mother dismissed her with a brusque wave of the hand and told her not to make such a fuss over an insignificant injury. She also recalled being scolded at the doctor's office because she was terrified of getting an injection. Her mother roughly pulled her out of the waiting room into an adjacent hallway where she spanked her for "being such a cry baby." From what she told me about her harsh mother, it became clear that young Lillian had never known the sweetness of the motherkiss that makes the bruised finger, the skinned knee, the feverish forehead, the frightened soul hurt less, and that she had never heard the mothervoice cooing, "I love you. I am here to make things better for you. You can lean on me."

As therapy progressed, Lillian helped me understand the emotional significance of the corporate position she was about to lose. More than well-paying and challenging, it provided her with a strong, sustaining support system. The secretaries and typists with whom she interacted daily were mostly older women who had taken her under their wing and nurtured her with a mothercare that she had never known—and that, all too soon, she would have to relinquish. Lillian's emotional crisis, which had at first bewildered me, now made a great deal of sense; indeed, Lillian was losing much and grieving was in order.

We agreed that after a necessary period of letting go and mourning, Lillian would be wise to cultivate relationships with nurturing, motherly women in her new workplace. (Friendships between people of different generations are often mutually enhancing; yet this form of relationship is rarely developed or celebrated in our society.) In the meantime, I offered my professional care and support. Several months into therapy, Lillian appeared at a session with a nasty case of flu. Coughing and wheezing, she cut short the hour in order to go home to bed. As she was about to leave, she smiled shyly and asked if I could tell her how to make chicken soup—and, smiling back (aware that this was an unconventional intervention indeed) I proceeded to give her the recipe that my own nurturing mother-in-law had, many years before, passed on to me.

In addition to cultivating a support system in her new workplace, Lillian would also have to develop a good *inner* mother on whom she could depend for soothing. Although she would not be able to model this inner mother after her flesh-and-blood mother, as more fortunate daughters do, she could create her out of the fragments of loving care that she had received from several people who had crossed her path—the motherly women at work, for example, as well as the therapist who had taught her how to make chicken soup. (In later chapters of this book, we will explore in greater detail how wounded adults successfully draw on past and present nurturing relationships to compensate for the less than adequate parenting they received as children.) Lillian and I are still working together, and I look on with delight as she becomes more self-loving.

Lillian's earlier solutions—drinking and compulsive eating—to assuage the distresses of everyday living are, as we all know, common escapes. Certainly, addictions are complicated disorders with many tangled roots, but my clinical experience suggests that women who as children did not receive adequate parental care are more susceptible to them than are their well-nurtured counterparts.[12]

For some, alcohol—which warms, fills, and anesthetizes the inner emptiness or aching—becomes the soothing mother: The bottle of wine replaces the bottle of formula;

the alcoholic stupor replaces the sensations of being wafted to a sound sleep in mother's arms. For others, food represents the nourishing mother. And for others still, the sexual partner is compensation for the absent soothing mother. As Lana, whose own mother died shortly after she was born, related, "Two or three nights a week, I go to The Broken Drum, a single's bar, to pick up a partner. It doesn't really matter who he is—tall, short; smart, dumb. In the act of love, my partner sews me back together; his caresses, his closeness make me feel secure—if only for a few minutes. Most of the other time, I feel as if I'm coming apart at the seams." For me, Lana's feeling of anxiety conjures the image of a tiny baby full of anxiety, limbs flailing, who is desperate to be held fast in a mother's arms.

The fortunate daughters who, during childhood, receive enough nurture tend to learn, as they grow up, to soothe themselves. For this reason they are less likely to turn to alcohol, compulsive eating, or compulsive sex for comfort. Instead, when they are in crisis—rejected by a lover or friend, overwhelmed by responsibilities at work, suffering the loss of good health or a job—they can turn to their good inner mother for comfort.

Recently I read an English folktale about a king, a beggar, and a monkey.[13] For ten years, the king sat in his chamber to hear petitions and dispense justice. Each day a holy man in the robe of a beggar appeared and without a word, offered him a piece of fruit. Although he always accepted the trifling gift, the king did not give it any thought but merely passed it on to his treasurer, who later tossed it from an upper trellised window into a neglected corner of the treasure house.

One day, ten years after the first appearance of the beggar, a tame monkey, which had escaped from the women's apartments in the inner palace, came bounding into the king's chamber and jumped onto the throne. Because the king had just received the beggar's fruit, he playfully handed it over to the monkey. When the monkey bit into it, a sparkling jewel dropped out and rolled onto the floor.

His eyes growing wide, the king turned to his treasurer and asked what had become of the beggar's many other gifts of fruit. Excusing himself, the treasurer went to the treasure house and made his way to the area directly under the trellised window, which he had not visited all these years. There, on the floor, lay a mass of fruit in various stages of decomposition and, amidst their remains, a heap of priceless gems.

This tale suggests that the most common gifts hold the most precious treasures. Although the early mother's soothing words ("Shhh, now there, everything will be just fine") and her countless acts of care (cradling, stroking, rocking, nursing; kissing the bruised little finger that got caught in the kitchen drawer; carrying the little one to bed so carefully that her feet won't dangle or bump against the furniture; making up stories about good fairies and guardian angels) are as commonplace as the beggar's offerings of fruit, they are also the priceless jewels of our core.

Daughters deprived of a nurturing flesh-and-blood mother can, however, become their own good mother—a self-soothing inner presence. One of my clients told me that sometimes when she is very upset she soaks in a warm bath—what better symbol of the holding mother?—and gradually relaxes and that at other times she snuggles in her cozy bed, pulls the down covers over her, and feels contained. Another, the mother of two little girls, explains that she assumes the same gentle attitude with herself that she assumes with a child in distress: "I talk to myself just as I would talk with one of my daughters if she were having a bad day. I tell myself not to get all worked up, that everything will be okay, and that I'm a good person even when I made a bad mistake." Still another shares that for as long as she can remember, the image of the Virgin Mary—unconditionally loving, giving, and life-affirming—has provided her comfort and a sense of her own lovableness; deprived of an enhancing flesh-and-blood mother, this client turns to a spiritual mother and internalizes her goodness.[14]

*     *     *

Just as children grow and change, so do their needs for mothercare. As the years pass and daughters venture into the world, they require a different kind of maternal protection. In addition to nurturing and soothing, the daughter needs her mother to shield her from destructive outsiders against whom she is defenseless: a bullying playmate, a sadistic teacher, or a violent neighbor, for example. When I was about ten, my mother noticed that I stiffened in the presence of our building superintendent, a frightful-looking man with facial lesions and a scarlet nose, who smelled of liquor and stale tobacco. She asked if he had ever tried to touch me and I told her no. Nevertheless, respecting my fear that he was somehow threatening, she put a protective arm around me whenever he appeared and also let me know that I should not ride alone in the elevator with him. Not only did my mother offer her physical protection but she also encouraged me to trust my intuition about the danger this man posed and to protect myself against him.

My client Faith tells me that in high school she went steady with a terribly wounded boy who began beating her. Innocent and trusting, she thought that her love would heal the young man and so she stayed with him. Her experienced mother, however, knew otherwise; she took legal action to ensure that the boy did not set foot in their house and, despite my client's rage at her, forbade the relationship. Although at the time Faith was convinced her mother was the wicked Witch of the West, she is now immensely grateful for her relentless, fierce, and loving maternal protectiveness.

In certain situations, a daughter needs her mother to protect her not only from outsiders but from insiders who threaten her well-being: a family member who is violent, alcoholic, or who exhibits sexually inappropriate behaviors, for example. Her loyalties strained, however, not every mother provides her daughter with the protection she deserves. A young woman tells me that when she was small, her emotionally disturbed sister repeatedly battered her.

Rolling up the sleeve of her sweater, she exposes a badly scarred arm and, in a matter-of-fact voice, reports that her sister had once flung a kettle of boiling water at her. When I ask how her parents reacted to this abuse, my client shrugs and remembers that they simply told her to be understanding and forgiving of her sister. What my client needed from her parents, however, was the assurance that they would do everything in their power to protect her against the sister's violence.

A friend in her middle years tells me that when she was little, her father, an alcoholic, told her dirty jokes that repulsed her; that he dragged her to sleazy bars where drunks sidled up to her, made off-color remarks, and left her feeling somehow violated; and that since her mother did not try to stop the father's inappropriate behavior, she felt betrayed by both parents—feelings that are with her even now. In a similar vein, an adolescent client reveals that her father, though not overtly incestuous, behaves in a sexually inappropriate manner—is a little too concerned with the way she looks, a little too romantic with her when they are out together, a little too affectionate, a little too jealous of her boyfriends—and that her mother, rather than addressing the father's seductive behavior and attempting to put a stop to it, ignores or makes light of it, leaving her daughter emotionally abandoned.

The most extreme failure of maternal protection involves the sexual exploitation of a child by a trusted adult. Research shows that without capable and involved mothers to safeguard them, daughters are in great jeopardy of being sexually preyed upon, even in their own homes, even by their own fathers.[15] The sexual exploitation of the motherless girl (motherlessness may be either a physical or a psychological state) is not a modern phenomenon; sadly, it has a long tradition.

Indeed, the earliest versions of the Cinderella story—so different from the Walt Disney adaptation—tell about a maiden who, after her mother's death, is preyed upon by her sex-starved father.[16] It is the spirit of the dead mother— symbolized by a little hazelnut tree—that offers solace and aid to the threatened girl, thus safeguarding her chastity. In the Christian version of Cinderella, the legend of Saint Dympna, the motherless Dympna is not so fortunate. Despite valiant efforts, she is never safe from her father, who has fallen in love with her because she resembles his deceased wife. Although she flees across the ocean in disguise, he pursues her relentlessly until he finds her. Refusing to submit to his sexual demands, Dympna is beheaded by the cruel man.

A recent book by Louise DeSalvo, *Virginia Woolf*, traces the impact of incest and parental neglect on Woolf's life and work.[17] What emerges from DeSalvo's study is a portrait of a woman who, throughout her life—in the stories she wrote as a little girl, in letters to family members and friends, in the journal she kept as an adolescent, in her novels, and finally in an unfinished autobiography, "A Sketch of the Past"—called attention to the plight of unprotected children. Virginia Woolf was perhaps the first to give the neglected, sexually exploited girl child a full voice—and it speaks of deep sadness, self-hatred, helplessness, and fear.

In "A Sketch of the Past," Woolf details her abuse, in her own home, by family members, most conspicuously her half-brother Gerald Duckworth, from the time she was six and for many years thereafter. Understanding that sexual abuse was probably the central and most formative feature of her early years, she recalls a sense of not being connected to her own experience, of living behind a screen, "the feeling . . . of lying in a grape and seeing through a film of semi-transparent yellow,"[18] of being wrapped in cotton wool, of being deadened and sometimes disembodied.

Like so many other mothers who do not protect their daughters from sexual exploitation by a family member, Virginia Woolf's mother, Julia Stephen, probably did not intend harm. Her inadequacy as a parent derived mainly from acts of omission—inadvertent neglect. "Can I remember ever being alone with her for more than a few minutes?" Virginia once wrote in a letter to her sister.[19] As the prototypic Angel of the House who tried to serve the needs of too many people—her emotionally draining husband, her demanding mother, her house guests, the young men who flattered her, the poor—she could not also look after her three daughters, each of whom was sexually molested. In the process of sacrificing herself, Julia also sacrificed her daughters. Indeed, for Virginia, mother was never more than a "general presence."[20]

Judith Lewis Herman writes in her landmark study, *Father-Daughter Incest:* "The personal accounts of incest victims are replete with descriptions of distant, unavailable mothers and with expressions of longing for maternal nurturance."[21] In fact, it is the neglected daughter's craving for closeness and affection that makes her even more vulnerable to the sexual advances of an outsider. Unlike Virginia Woolf's contemporary Colette, who wrote about sheltering mothergardens with ripe, growing fruits and vegetables, Woolf described herself as a little plant that grew without care or cultivation. In *A Cockney's Farming Experience*, a novel written when she was ten, she tells how it feels never to have enough food— the symbol of maternal nourishment: The cockney [the husband] goes out to milk the cow and after "an hour's hard work managed to get about a half an inch of milk at the bottom of the milk jug." Harriet [the wife] tries to boil the only two eggs which they have, but they turn out to be "as hard as bricks."[22]

It was in large part Woolf's determination to make sense of her lifelong depression that led her to write "A Sketch of the Past" and to remember and record what had been done to her as a child: "Only when we put two and two together— two pencil strokes, two written words . . . do we overcome dissolution."[23] However, journeying in solitude to explore her psyche and uncovering the previously repressed memories of her sexual abuse as well as the general violence that had permeated the Stephen household triggered feelings that overwhelmed her. Without support and affirmation from others, Woolf began to disbelieve her own experience, to discount the legitimacy of her anguish, to hold herself responsible for what had been done to her, to think herself crazy. Moreover, as she came to doubt the fundamental accuracy of her long-term memory, she also came to deny the significant neglect by her parents. Describing them not as they were but as she wished them to be, she wrote: "How beautiful they were those old people—I mean father and mother. . . . How serene & gay & even their life reads to me: No mud; no whirlpools. And so human—with the children & the little hum and song of the nursery."[24] Before completing "A Sketch of the Past," Virginia Woolf drowned herself.

When a woman begins to put two and two together, to recognize that the parents in whom she placed all her child's trust betrayed her, she may feel that she is coming apart. The revelation that her own mother did not care enough to safeguard her or, in extreme cases, that she *intentionally* caused her pain can crush the spirit, rupture an emotional bedrock—the certainty that mother always loved and valued her. When a woman begins to put two and two together, she may wish to bury what she is bringing up, just as she did as a child: Is it not safer to deny, suppress, or minimize the truth than to risk destroying the ideal of the loving parent? However, in order for the woman neglected or abused as a child to heal, her truth must be exposed, must be felt (as painful as the experience is), must be put into words, and must be listened to and affirmed by at least one other empathic, accepting human being. In her determination to overcome the effects of incest, Virginia Woolf met all these conditions except the last.

The basic need for human comfort in the healing process is beautifully illustrated in an old Hasidic tale.[25] There once was an inquisitive and bold rabbi who asked the Lord to teach him about Heaven and Hell. The Lord agreed to help the rabbi out and decided to instruct him first about Hell.

To this end, He escorted the rabbi to a room where a group of starving, miserable men was sitting around a large table. In the middle of the table sat a bowl of rich, nourishing soup and next to it a ladle with a very long handle. Time and again, the starving men had tried to feed themselves by dipping the ladle into the soup but, despite their manipulations, had discovered that because the handle was so long, they could never guide it into their hungry mouths. The full pot sitting in the middle of the round table was a constant reminder of the starving men's helplessness and eternal misery: Surely this was Hell.

Now the Lord was ready to show the rabbi Heaven. He escorted him to a room just like the first where another group of men was also sitting around a large table. In the middle of the table sat a comparable pot of thick soup and next to it a long-handled ladle. But the men in this room were well-nourished and happy. You see, they had learned to feed each other.

In my practice, I have encountered many wounded women who, never having known appropriate maternal protection and nurturance, do not at first trust human comfort and support. And I suspect that there are countless others who do not seek help from a therapist, a support group, or anyone else for that matter, because they are convinced that they should depend only on themselves—just as they have always done. It is true that we cannot undo our past. A woman who as a young child was insufficiently mothered can never fully make up what she missed. But if—despite our inclinations not to trust or need people—we take a chance and open ourselves up just a bit, we may find that others understand our loss and that in being understood we are somehow soothed. Accepting from a kindly hand a ladle full of rich, warm soup, we may discover how nourishing it is.

# CHAPTER 4

# The Harm of
# Possessive Love

Mother clings to me. She murmurs vaguely that
she has lost her little girl. Of life, which has been
all hardness and pain for her, she expected a sole
compensation, and she does not even have that.
. . . There are times when, in horror of the grief
I am causing the mother I love beyond words, I
think myself mad. . . . And Mother sees in our
separation only the ruin of all her dreams, her
hopes, her needs, her very life.

—Anaïs Nin
*Journal of a Wife*

"Oh, you wicked child, what do you say? I
thought I had separated you from all the world,
and yet you have deceived me." In her rage she
seized Rapunzel's beautiful hair, twisted it twice
round her left hand, snatched up a pair of shears,
and cut off the plaits, which fell to the ground.

—Brothers Grimm
"Rapunzel"

On my way to work, I sometimes stop to browse
in a wonderful shop that sells out-of-print books and art
prints. On my last visit, I came across an old steel engraving
of a painting by A. Bourland, a nineteenth-century French
painter, entitled "The Prisoner." It is a portrait of a tender
young woman cradling a white-feathered bird, which seems
to be more child than animal. On first glance, the woman
appears to be nurturing the little creature in her charge, but

then one notices that the bird-child is struggling to set itself free from her hold and that the caressive maternal hand is also strangulating.

Just as the good mother nurtures and protects her young, she also prepares them to leave her sheltering realm—her protective nest—and to venture out into the world without her. For many mothers, however, "letting go" poses great difficulties, and, like the beautiful woman of the Bourland painting, they do not willingly release their children from their hold. Similarly, for many daughters, being let go creates such anxiety that they are unwilling to separate from mother and become individuals in their own right. In this chapter we will focus on leavetakings between mother and daughter and look at the ways failures of separation cripple a daughter's growth.

The resistance toward loosening the mother-daughter bond is illuminated in a bizarre but true story, upon which Erich Hackl bases his historical novel, *Aurora's Motive*. Aurora Rodriquez was a brilliant feminist raised in the oppressive and provincial milieu of early twentieth-century Spain. Prevented from pursuing a career, Aurora was determined to raise a child who would live out her own stunted aspirations. Unmarried, she advertised in the newspaper for a man to impregnate her and selected from the respondents a renegade priest, who readily agreed to forfeit any relationship with their future child. In due time, Aurora gave birth to a daughter, Hildegart, whom she raised with total devotion.

Hildegart proved to be the extraordinary child of Aurora's dreams—the precious jewel in her crown. For example, the wunderkind won a typing proficiency certificate from the Underwood typewriter firm at age three. And, beginning her studies in law at Madrid's Central University at thirteen, she was soon famous as an activist and writer of feminist radical doctrine. Indeed, shaped by Aurora, the girl became known as the "Valkyrie of the New Era."

Throughout Hildegart's childhood and early adolescence, she and her mother were inseparable; not only did they spend an inordinate amount of time together—Hildegart was not permitted playmates—but they were also of one mind. As time went on, however, the once-compliant Hildegart began to draw away from her mother by asserting differences from her. Despite Aurora's objections, Hildegart wanted to choose her own clothes, and in an obvious attempt to attract the attentions of young men, she bedecked herself with bracelets, necklaces, and brooches. In addition, Hildegart, who in the past had shared every thought with her mother, became secretive and, as worrisome for Aurora, assumed a new carefree attitude, a joie de vivre that contradicted her former studiousness and uncompromising responsibility. Aurora, profoundly threatened, could not contemplate an end to the unity with her daughter, her life's devotion. Instead of accepting their differences and normal separation, she interpreted her daughter's spirited individuality as a sign of defectiveness inherited from the man who fathered her.

The tension between Aurora and Hildegart peaked when the seventeen-year-old girl came under the influence of the eminent novelist and social activist H. G. Wells, who invited her to leave Spain and work for him and his well-known friend Havelock Ellis in London. Torn between the role of devoted superdaughter and longings for her own life's adventures, Hildegart turned to her mother for advice. In an attempt to reach a peaceful resolution, the two women locked themselves in a room for two days without sleep. During this time, Aurora convinced Hildegart that her filial disloyalty and deviations from the straight and narrow were signs of unforgivable corruption. Accepting these harsh judgments, Hildegart became despondent and, seeing no solution, begged Aurora to kill her; Aurora, ever the devoted mother, complied. She was consequently found guilty of murder by gunshot, sentenced to a 26-year prison term, and eventually transferred to a mental institution, where she died in 1955.

Aurora and Hildegart provide an extreme and pathological example of failed separation; yet when we overlook their grotesque final solution, we can find similarities between them and countless ordinary mother-daughter pairs. Deprived of a full life of her own—as so many women in past generations have been—Aurora suffered an inner emptiness. By defining and possessing Hildegart's life, she compensated for her own unrealized one. Investing all in Hildegart, Aurora could not allow her a life of her own, for without her daughter to live through she would be nothing. Rather, Aurora perceived the child as a valued extension of herself— the jewel in her plain crown, which she safeguarded, as one would keep a rare treasure in a vault, by insulating her from outsiders (her father, mentors, potential friends, and romantic partners). Blind to her selfish motives—as grandiose or supermothers often are—Aurora did not recognize that she was "protecting" Hildegart more for her own benefit than for the child's. Before her death, Hildegart wrote,

> She wanted an offshoot of herself, a second Aurora, a happier, more successful self. I was supposed to be freer, more munificent, more courageous, capable of organizing things according to my, her, wishes. I was to be strong, clever, creative, and also engaging, everything she herself failed in.[1]

Fairy-tale characters exaggerate and thereby illuminate traits that are prevalent among human beings. The needy and possessive Aurora finds a parallel in the character of the sorceress from "Rapunzel" by the Brothers Grimm. During Rapunzel's early years, the sorceress appears to be a caring mother figure, for the radiant and sweet Rapunzel thrives in her charge. But when the girl turns twelve, the sorceress mother becomes justifiably afraid that she will soon lose her to an outsider. In order to preserve their exclusive relationship, she locks the girl in a high tower, where only she is allowed visitation. For a long time, mother and daughter are entwined by Rapunzel's splendid long tresses, but then one day the beautiful girl lets down her hair for a stranger, the prince with whom she falls in love. Made mean by her jealous love, the sorceress mother viciously puts an end to their tender liaison.

Most villainous fairy-tale mothers face terrible punishments for their foul deeds: Birds peck out the eyes of Cinderella's abusive stepmother, and Snow White's murderously envious stepmother dances to her death in red-hot shoes. Interestingly, no harm befalls the sorceress. Child psychiatrist Bruno Bettelheim explains that Rapunzel, who represents all daughters, has a basic sympathy for her. Despite the mother's excesses, Rapunzel believes that the old woman cares deeply about her, that she acts out of too much love—foolish and selfish as it is—rather than out of wickedness.

It is the very fact, however, that the jealously possessive, overprotective mother is devoted that makes it so hard for daughters to separate from her. Hildegart, for example, was unable to condemn her mother's exclusive hold on her. She knew that her mother was persecuting her young life, but she also knew that her mother was a victim, that Aurora's possessiveness was the result of a deep wounding. To claim her own life, to defy the mother to whom she was *everything*, were burdens with which she could not live. Better to die than to live in ways that would cause pain and bring disappointment to the one who loved her best of all. Moreover, strongly identified with her mother, Hildegart had absorbed the older woman's basic mistrust of the world at large. Threatened by her own impulses to become self-sufficient and separate from her protective mother, she found it safer to die than to face the dangerous world alone.

Unlike Hildegart, Rapunzel does succeed in leaving her mother—but only after considerable inner conflict. Bettelheim notes that because Rapunzel knows how important she is to her sorceress mother (and, let me add, how important her sorceress mother is to her), she undermines their impending separation: Guilty about her clandestine meetings with the prince and the fact that he is now the one she loves most, ambivalent about leaving the caretaking mother, Rapunzel makes one of the rare Freudian slips in folk literature, thereby spilling her secret as she asks the unsuspecting sorceress, "Tell me, Mother Gothel, how can it be that you are so much heavier to draw up than the young prince who will be here before long?"[2] As Rapunzel no doubt anticipates, her sorceress mother becomes enraged when she learns about the prince's secret visits and does all she can to prevent an elopement.

Were Rapunzel at peace in leaving mother for her prince, she would not set herself up for punishment. And her punishment for separating is severe indeed. Not only does the sorceress mother clip Rapunzel's beautiful long tresses, but she evicts her from the tower that is home and leaves her in the wilderness, where for years the suffering girl endures poverty and the pain of loss before she is reunited with her prince. As the wise fairy tale teaches, mother-daughter separations are fraught with anguish and both mothers and daughters resist leaving one another.

In my practice, I frequently encounter daughters who, like Rapunzel and Hildegart, cannot easily separate—either in a physical or psychological sense—from the mothers who hold them fast. Although the separation struggle between mothers and daughters is most dramatic during the push and pull years of adolescence, it continues—often in disguised forms—throughout adulthood. The following four vignettes are representative of the many accounts of unsatisfactory separations that come to my attention.

Patricia is a forty-two-year-old client who describes herself as a dutiful daughter who was brought up by strict Catholic parents. For the past five months, however, she has hidden from her mother, Mary, the fact that she is living with a man who is separated but not divorced from his wife. Patricia's cover-up is time-consuming and emotionally draining: Before each visit from mother, she carefully stores away her partner's clothes and personal belongings; whenever mother inquires about her social activities, she is forced to make up lies. Yet, despite the toll these deceptions exact, Patricia is unwilling to reveal her situation, afraid that neither she nor Mary could withstand their strongly opposed values: "Mother makes it very clear that I am her favorite because we are so much alike. She looks down at my sister, who is a free spirit of sorts. I sometimes think that if Mother knew about my love affair with a married man, she would die of a broken heart. Other times I think she would be angry enough to disown me."

Although she has a responsible job as a production manager, thirty-year-old Nellie continues to live with her mother, Kitty, with whom she does not get along. During sessions, Nellie complains endlessly about the older woman's nasty ways and agrees with me that it would make sense to find her own lodgings (both she and her mother are healthy and financially secure), yet she takes no steps to move out. Knowing how dependent Kitty is—even as a young child, Nellie was effectively her mother's mother—Nellie believes their long overdue separation would be a cruel desertion: "It is true that my mother is mostly unpleasant with me. But if eyes could speak, hers would say, 'Don't leave me; without you I'll die.' Strange as it seems, I think I would miss her a lot too. We've grown so used to each other."

During childhood and adolescence, Robin had lovingly tended her chronically ill mother, Rose—bringing her hot tea and toast with marmalade, sitting at the foot of her bed sharing funny stories about school or work, listening to records with her. Indeed, Robin became the loving companion that her mother's preoccupied, workaholic husband never was. Then, at age twenty-one, Robin married—leaving home and Rose. Although Rose did not outwardly disapprove of the marriage, she never accepted her new son-in-law as "family." For her part, Robin had the vague sense that by marrying, she was betraying mother, breaking up their sacred union. Within a short time after the marriage, Robin developed physical symptoms that mimicked Rose's, which, after three years of various medical treatments, have not abated. As if punishing herself for physically leaving mother, Robin seems to have created, through their shared pain, a new fusion with her.

Twenty-six-year-old Sharon describes her mother, Ernestine, as loving and extremely generous and berates herself for often feeling irritated with her. During therapy, we come to understand that Ernestine's generosity is an inadvertent form of tyranny. For example, she insists on buying clothes for her daughter, and although Sharon does not share her mother's taste, she wears the outfits Ernestine picks out so as not to hurt her feelings. Moreover, Ernestine never visits Sharon's new apartment without still another housewarming gift in hand: The walls are hung with *mother's* favorite Renoir prints, the breakfront displays the china cups *mother* could not resist buying, the bathroom overflows with the fuscia towels *mother* simply adores. Although she is self-supporting and lives in her own place, Sharon cannot shake free of mother.

Each of the daughters I have discussed has not yet asserted her right to be separate and different, to say to her mother (and to herself), "I love you, Mother, and am grateful for all you've provided for me. You have helped make me strong. Now it is time to assert my own will, to be my own self, to live apart, to let you go so that I can move on." In emotional terms, each pays a heavy price for failing to separate from mother.

Patricia is tense living her double life; instead of being adult and self-assured, she feels like a naughty child always on the verge of getting caught. Moreover, each time she makes up a lie about her love relationship, she loses a little piece of her integrity and is cheapened.

Nellie is troubled by conflicting feelings of obligation toward her mother and fears of becoming independent of her. Although she feels suffocated sharing quarters with her and wants to be free, she has also become comfortable in their unhealthy relationship. Just as Nellie is unsure that mother can live without her, Nellie does not have the confidence that she can survive without mother.

Worn out by chronic aches and pains, Robin cannot participate in life joyfully. Furthermore, because she shares her mother's belief that leaving her for a man was a betrayal, she undermines her love relationship by maintaining an emotional and sexual distance from her husband. Fused to mother, she remains, in one sense, an unmarried woman, a faithful child.

And Sharon, afraid of hurting mother's feelings, does not allow herself the joy of autonomy. Mother still dresses her up and decorates her living space, just as she did when her daughter lived at home. The material things that are an extension of mother are constant reminders of her omnipotence and of her hold on Sharon. Always indebted to Ernestine for her generosity, Sharon is not aware that her gnawing anger at the older woman is a legitimate protest against her inadvertent tyranny. Instead, Sharon savages herself for being an ungrateful daughter.

Certainly these four mother-daughter pairs are not enmeshed in relationships as poisonous as the one between Hildegart and Aurora. Yet they seem to share the belief that it is immoral, heartless, disloyal, or dangerous for mothers and daughters to take leave of each other. Surely, part of every daughter wants to stay safe with mother forever; after all, the world beyond mother's sheltering realm is not always gentle and kind. In addition, part of every daughter wants to be a sweet comfort and constant companion to mother, just as she was during childhood. When a mother colludes with the daughter's regressive tendencies to remain her special girl, however, as Mary, Kitty, Rose, and Ernestine do, she reduces her to a child.

Most people shake their heads in disapproval when a grown son remains tied to his mother, contemptuously labeling him a "Mama's boy." Yet the same people who deride an unseparated relationship between mother and son are likely not to challenge a similarly intense attachment between mother and daughter. In our culture, the belief persists that optimal relationships between mother and daughter are indeed very, very close.

> A son is a son 'til he takes a wife,
> But a daughter's a daughter the rest of her life.[3]

To be sure, after the sturm und drang of early adolescence, the most fortunate mothers and daughters do enjoy a warm and loving relationship, but becoming best friends is not in their interest. Rather than best friends, the most fortunate mothers and daughters become cross-generational friends who, by virtue of their different stages in life, necessarily have a certain distance between them. Always a generation ahead, the wisest mothers lay paths for their daughters that the daughters may choose to follow. As one of my clients said recently, "My eighty-five-year-old mother is bedridden and terminally ill, but although I feed and clean her, she is still my mentor. Watching her die with dignity intact, I think I will also be prepared to die this way."

Conversely, mothers who act as their daughters' peers dissolve the desirable boundaries between them and forfeit their roles as guides. I am presently treating a bulimic college student whose best girlfriend is her mother. In addition to sharing clothes, jewelry, and make-up, they also toy with the idea of sharing boyfriends. When she began treatment, Bunnie defended their relationship: "I don't have any problems with my mother. I've never wanted to rebel or separate from her because she doesn't act like a mom." Over time, however, her deep resentments surfaced. With a mother who is her equal and her chum, who is as confused about life as she is, Bunnie feels lost. As she was able to articulate recently, "Because my mother refuses to take the lead and walk ahead of me, I don't know where I'm supposed to be going." In order for Bunnie to thrive, she requires a mother who is mature enough to separate from her, to grow into her own age rather than to stay fixated at her daughter's.

In my experience, mothers and daughters who are able to grow apart are, paradoxically, best able to come together. When a person does not expect to be encompassed by another, she can let down her guard and allow a closeness to develop between them. If her autonomy and selfness are not threatened by an intrusive mother, a daughter can feel safe being close to her. The daughter who is not afraid to be separate from her mother may also find it easier to develop healthy, separated relationships with other women.[4]

I am reminded of my own relationship with my friend Susan and of a special moment we recently shared in the mountain woods. Four or five times a year Susan and I retreat for the weekend to a cabin in Estes Park, where we work many hours on our separate writing projects but where we also prepare meals together, take walks, and have long conversations. One time, as we were gathering dried plants, small stones, and red pine cones at sunset, we encountered a mother deer and her newborn. For several minutes, the four of us were motionless. Then trusting that we would not violate their sacred space by coming too close, the doe nursed her fawn as we two human mothers stood by in appreciation and awe. What Susan and I have come to understand is that by respecting each other's needs for privacy and solitude—just as we naturally kept a distance from the deer—we nurture our friendship; paradoxically, our separateness allows our intimacy.

Each of us has a right to a protected sacred space. When mothers and daughters are overly close, neither can breathe, move, expand. In past ages, the archetypal "destroyer mother" who squashes the child's need to grow apart has been represented by gruesome images: She is the vulture, the crow, the raven; she is Medusa flashing her petrifying gaze; the death-dealing goddess Kali; the terrible Gorgon with boar's tusks and outthrust tongues; and the monster of the deep sea whose crablike appendages grab hold and never let go. In our time, she is Mrs. Bates, the murderer mother in the movie *Psycho*, who, even in death, holds on to her grown son with an iron grip.

The human counterpart of the destroyer mother is the possessive mother who does not let go of her children. Although, in reality, the possessive mother is often emotionally frail and dependent, to the daughter in her grip she feels like a preying bird or devouring monster or soul murderess. One of my clients, a vibrant and successful woman, vividly describes the effects of her possessive mother.

Whenever my mother, who lives out of state, visits me I get physically ill. My body, which is normally relaxed, becomes like steel; my throat tightens; I can't breathe; my stomach churns. Rationally, I know my mother can't take me over. But something inside me is terrified of her, afraid of being pulled back into her life. My mother is not overly demanding or clutching, but, worse still, she always has this look of hungry expectancy—as if she's somehow waiting for me to fill her up. If I am not on my guard, keeping her at an arm's distance, I have the feeling that she will *eat me up*, and I will become part of her again—part of the void from which I have struggled so hard to free myself.

In her memoir, *Fierce Attachments*, Vivian Gornick writes about her widowed mother who, out of an extreme neediness and loneliness, drew the adolescent Vivian closer and closer, even requiring her to share the same bed. What is striking about Gornick's description is the visceral terror it evokes; we can feel with the young girl what it is like being sucked back into her mother's womb, the death womb.

My skin crawled with her. She was everywhere, all over me, inside and out. Her influence clung, membrane-like, to my nostrils, my eyelids, my open mouth. I drew her into me with every breath I took. I drowsed in her etherizing atmosphere, could not escape the rich and claustrophobic character of her presence, her being, her suffocating femaleness. . . . Her pain became my element, the country in which I lived, the rule beneath which I bowed. It commanded me, made me respond against my will. I longed endlessly to get away from her, but I could not leave the room when she was in it.[5]

It is not mere coincidence that Vivian and her mother grew overly close after the father's death. One of the roles of the good father is to act sometimes as buffer between his wife and daughter. By forming strong relationships with each, he prevents the pair from regressing to the state of oneness that marked their early bond. For the daughter, a strong, present father is also a precursor of the love partner who tempers her relationship to mother and eventually replaces mother as the one most loved. In Chapter 1, I described the enhancing mother as a reflective glass that affirms the child's beauty and goodness. Allow me to extend this metaphor: The enhancing father is sometimes the mirror's frame, which assures her of limits and boundaries. He shields the mother—his wife—from the small child's excessive demands for attention. And he shields the child from mothercare when it is excessive and therefore infantalizing and smothering. A colleague, Dr. Lyn Gulette, told me that when her small son tripped and skinned his knee, he came to her for tender loving care. After a short time, however, the boy said, "I think I'll go to Daddy now. I'm finished crying so I don't want to be with you anymore."

Lyn also lent me a wonderful children's book, which illuminates the different experiences mothers and fathers typically provide their children. In Maurice Sendak's *Outside Over There*, a little girl named Ida faces the terrors (represented by goblins, robbers, and kidnappers) of growing up.

To meet these challenges, she covers herself in her mother's
yellow rain cloak and climbs "backwards out of her window
into outside over there." As she whirls by dangerous robber
caves, she hears from the distant sea "her Sailor Papa's song:
'If Ida backwards in the rain / would only turn around
again / and catch those goblins with a tune / she'd spoil
their kidnap honeymoon!' "[6] And this is exactly what Ida
does. Surely, Mother's rain cloak offers protection, but in
order for Ida to become strong and competent she needs
more than mother's comfort—indeed, as Sendak implies, too
much of mother's loving protectiveness pulls the young girl
*backward* into babyhood. In Ida's case, it is her Sailor Papa's
song, which she plays on her own "wonder horn," that leads
her *forward* and enables her to become the "brave, bright
little Ida . . . for her Papa, who loves her always."[7]

Vivian Gornick was not so fortunate as little Ida. Without
her father to act as buffer between them, she and her emotionally needy mother developed a skintight attachment that
pulled them backward, not only during Vivian's adolescence
but throughout her adulthood. Vivian's desperate longing
to retrieve the lost father who would rescue her from mother's boundless presence is revealed in a dream.

One night when I was fifteen I dreamed that the entire
apartment was empty, stripped of furniture and brilliantly
whitewashed, the rooms gleaming with sun and the whiteness of walls. A long rope extended the length of the
apartment, winding at waist-level through all the rooms.
I followed the rope from my room to the front door. There
in the open doorway stood my dead father, gray-faced,
surrounded by mist and darkness, the rope tied around
the middle of his body. I laid my hands on the rope and
began to pull, but try as I might I could not lift him across
the threshold. Suddenly my mother appeared. She laid her
hands over mine and began to pull also. I tried to shake
her off, enraged at her interference, but she would not
desist, and I did so want to pull him in I said to myself,

"All right, I'll even let her have him, if we can just get him back inside."[8]

Fathers are absent from their daughter's life for any number of reasons. Some, such as Vivian's father, die; some desert their families, some, although physically present, are depressed or uninterested or preoccupied and withdraw emotionally so that they are hardly there; and some, unsure of themselves as parents, allow themselves to be pushed out of the family circle. In certain instances, women concerned about the daughter's well-being have little choice but to insulate her from her father: The alcoholic or drug-abusing father, the violent or exploitative one, pose too grave a danger to her. In other cases, however, women lock out the father without adequate justification and at great emotional expense to her.

Frequently mothers are fueled by an intense anger toward men brought on by past abuses. Those who have been mistreated by their own fathers, for example, may generalize their justifiable hatred for him toward all men. "To be perfectly honest with you, Dr. Bassoff," Arlene, who is married to a kind, well-meaning young man and pregnant with their first child, confides, "If my baby is a girl, I don't know if I'll feel safe leaving her with Bob. How can I be sure he won't molest her the way my grandfather molested me? How can I be sure he's trustworthy?" Arlene, troubled that she cannot trust her own husband, is in therapy to build a more loving relationship with him—for their sake and for the sake of their child. However, much like the militant Aurora Rodriguez, other women I have known willfully eliminate the father from their children's lives.

Recently, I had lunch with a bright, energetic, affluent professor in her late thirties who, except for the fact that she has not been able to make a lasting love relationship, seems to have everything going for her. My colleague told me that she has no interest whatsoever in marrying but wants a child and is in the process of deciding whether to adopt, go to a sperm bank, or find a man to impregnate her.[9] When I suggested that the fatherless child necessarily suffers a great loss, she stiffened and retorted, "*I* will provide my child with everything that she needs."

Some women exclude their daughter's father in more subtle ways. In my office, for example, I observe a young couple with their first child. Each time the new father attempts to care for the six-month-old girl—give her some finger food, quiet her down, distract her with a toy—his wife rolls her eyes and indicates that he is doing something wrong. Gradually he withdraws his attention from the baby. In a similar vein, a teenage client tells me, "As long as I can remember, my mother has always made a fool of my father. Everything he does where the family is concerned is 'stupid' or 'ridiculous.' I guess I learned to believe that my mother was the competent parent and that my father was nothing but a buffoon."

I remember as well that as a young, full-time mother I was also guilty of pushing my husband out of the warm little nest I shared with my baby daughter. Without an outside job, I began to assume that parenting Leah was my exclusive territory. The worst fight my husband and I ever had was precipitated by his feelings of exclusion. Seeing the "you're in our way" look on both of our faces, he ranted and railed, then stormed out of the house one New Year's Eve, half-threatening not to return. When he did come back hours later, he insisted on always having an involved and essential relationship with each of us. Through his pain, I came to understand that the enhancing mother and wife does not set out to exclude loving others from her daughter's life. Maternal love requires gradually *letting go* the exclusive relationship mother and infant daughter share by *letting in* other significant people—father, grandparents, aunts, uncles, teachers, and male and female friends.

In writing this chapter, I searched high and low for a example of the mother who does not try to possess her daughter. Ironically, I found it in my own backyard. My own mother made it easy for me to let in others and take leave of her. Wise enough to know that she could not provide all, she did not insist on an exclusive relationship. She was not jealous of the teachers who played such an important part in my life, nor of my grandmother who took over my care in order for her to work; she always liked my friends and made them feel welcome in our home, and when, at age twenty, I left her permanently to make a life with my husband, she sent me off with a hug and a smile and even approved of my close relationship to my mother-in-law. Thinking back, what I remember most vividly is her support of the warm and sustaining relationship I enjoyed with my father. When my mother's holding arms felt too enclosing and too familiar, I knew I was free to break out of them and enter his realm.

After school I often walked to Nasch's French Pastry Shop, where my parents were employed. I loved to watch my mother at work. One of seven salesladies, she could work the cash register and tie cake boxes faster than anyone else, and with her Viennese charm, she could placate the most cantankerous customer. Busy as she was, whenever I came to Nasch's, she stopped what she was doing, doted over me for a few minutes, and invited me to choose a treat from the display cases, which held trays of heart-shaped butter cookies, mocha cream puffs, strawberry shortcakes, slices of open-faced plum pie, and much more. Then, after I had my sweet, I asked if I could visit with my father in the bakery, and she always said yes, adding, "Ach, what a father you have! Believe me, Evi, men like him they don't make no more."

A swinging door separated the bakery from the rest of the store. Moving through it was like being blasted from a temperate zone into a tropical one. In the summertime, the temperature hovered around 110 degrees Fahrenheit. Like a punch in the stomach, the heat took my breath away and made my eyes sting, but after a few minutes I did not much mind it.

The bakers wore long white aprons and their sweaty faces

and arms were always dusted with flour. From kneading dough and carrying huge vats of cream, sugar, eggs and flour, they had developed wonderfully strong bodies, which I secretly admired and memorized. To this day, when I am afraid, I draw on the vision of my father's powerful muscled arms, which, as a child, I half believed could carry me away from all the bad in the world. Of course, the bakery was not a tropical paradise. The long work hours and unrelenting heat of the ovens aggravated the men's tempers and sometimes their flare-ups exploded into fist fights. But because the bakers genuinely liked each other and me, I was not worried by their outbursts. On the contrary, their flashes of temper and rowdiness, their jokes and pranks, which contrasted with the polite interactions of the salesladies and customers, exhilarated me. With the bakers, I was less reserved than usual, sometimes even sassy. When I was hungry, for example, I did not ask for a treat; I simply stuck out my tongue and waited for one of them to *schpritz* some buttercream or chocolate icing on it.

In the bakery, I learned that men had an energy—different from women's energy—that made me laugh hard and let loose; in the bakery, I learned to be comfortable among men and to like them. Here, under my father's eye, I also discovered the fun of competing, something my mother frowned upon. "Evi," she would say, "if you show boys you know as much as they do, you'll chase them all away." "Evi," my father would say playfully, "show me how smart you are!"

On one of my visits to the bakery, my father put me through a test. He sat me and my cousin Bobby, the owner's son, in front of two separate but identical trays of sponge cake, cut into numerous little squares. At my father's urging, the bakers placed bets on the cousin they thought would count the squares more quickly. My father, who was usually stingy with money, put three dollars on me, a vast sum I thought. As Bobby counted by twos, which took a long time, I multiplied the number of squares on the periphery of the tray and came up quickly with the right answer. The bakers applauded me, my father made sure that everyone knew I was only in third grade and already a "math whiz," smiled his sweet smile, and collected his money, while I swelled with new self-confidence.

"*Je suis un autre*," the poet Rimbaud writes; "I am an other." My father was the first "other" who invited me, many years ago, to leave the realm of mother—warm, familiar, enclosing—and take in the world outside her. With his guidance, *with her blessings*, I was allowed to become separate and different from her: to become an other.

I would like to conclude this chapter on separation with an excerpt from a parable by the early twentieth-century South African writer Olive Schreiner, which I came across in Madonna Kolbenschlag's book *Lost in the Land of Oz*. Although the parable is about a mother and son, it can easily be applied to mother and daughter. It tells of a woman coming out of the desert in search of the Land of Freedom and of the guide she encounters, a father figure by the name of Reason, who enables her to relinquish her hold on her child so that both of them can grow stong and free. Interestingly, here, as in the Bourland engraving I described at the beginning of this chapter, the child has the form of a bird. But in this case, his mother's caressive hand is empowering, not strangulating.

> And she said, "I am ready; let me go."
> And he said, "No—but stay; what is at your breast?"
> She was silent.
> He said, "Open it and let me see."
> And she opened her garment. And against her breast was a tiny thing, who drank from it, and the yellow curls above his forehead pressed against it; and his knees were drawn up to her, and he held her breast fast with his hands.
> And Reason said, "Who is he and what is he doing here?"

And she said, "See his little wings . . ."

And Reason said, "Put him down."

And she said, "He is asleep, and he is drinking! I will carry him to the Land of Freedom. He has been a child so long, so long, I have carried him. In the Land of Freedom he will be a man. We will walk together there, and his great white wings will overshadow me. He has lisped one word only to me in the desert—"Passion!" I have dreamed he might learn to say 'Friendship' in that land."

And Reason said, "Put him down!"

And she said, "I will carry him so—with one arm, and with the other I will fight the water."

He said, "Lay him down on the ground. When you are in the water you will forget to fight, you will think only of him. "Lay him down," He said. "He will not die. When he finds you have left him alone he will open his wings and fly. He will be in the Land of Freedom before you. . . . He will be a man then, not a child. At your breast he cannot thrive; put him down that he may grow."

And she took her bosom from his mouth, and he bit her, so that the blood ran down on the ground. And she laid him down on the earth; and she covered her wound. And she bent and stroked his wings.[10]

# PART II

 *New Realities*

The little girl gave a cry of amazement and looked about her, her eyes growing bigger and bigger at the wonderful sights she saw.

The cyclone had set the house down, very gently—for a cyclone—in the midst of a country of marvelous beauty.

—L. Frank Baum
*The Wizard of Oz*

# CHAPTER 5

# *Revisiting the Land of Oz*

"Is your name Dorothy, my dear?"

"Yes," answered the child drying her tears. . . .

"Then you must go to the City of Emeralds. . . ."

"How can I get there?" asked Dorothy.

"You must walk. It is a long journey, through a country that is sometimes pleasant and sometimes dark and terrible. . . ."

—L. Frank Baum
*The Wizard of Oz*

When I was a little girl, my grandmother and I shared a special ritual. Each morning I crawled into her bed, snuggled next to her, and asked for a story. Grandma never disappointed; she created marvelous tales about handsome princes and beautiful princesses, talking animals, and flowers with human feelings. Kind, brave, and true, the characters in Grandma's stories, who faced and triumphed over all sorts of dangers and hardships, became my trusted guides, my secret friends. Although she died several years ago, my grandmother's love and respect for the imaginary are a part of me, and just as when I was small, fairy tales and folktales enchant me and deepen my understanding of human behavior.

So when a friend of mine pointed out that L. Frank Baum's *The Wizard of Oz*, on which the famous movie is based, can be seen as a story about woundings and healings in the mother-daughter relationship, I wasted no time reading it.[1] Although Baum indicated that his only purpose in writing was to delight young audiences, his work proves to be much more than entertainment for children. Indeed, the story of Dorothy Gale, the little girl from Kansas, describes a journey that every daughter who has been wounded by her mother makes in order to become whole. While at first glance, Dorothy's bigger-than-life adventures in the magical Land of Oz appear unrelated to the tasks ordinary women face, by decoding the symbolic language of this modern American folktale, one can find much with which to identify and from which to learn.

Dorothy Gale is twice wounded. Her first mother physically abandons her, leaving Dorothy an orphan, and her second mother, Aunt Em, cannot provide the child with a nurturing environment. Indeed, Baum describes Dorothy's childhood in Kansas as mostly gray—the color associated with depression, inertia, and indifference. The great treeless prairie of plowed fields and grasses blanched by the sun is gray; the Gales' house, its paint blistered by summers of hot sun and washed away by years of rain, is gray; even Dorothy's stern and silent Uncle Henry, from his scraggly beard to his heavy boots, is gray. But worst of all is Aunt Em's grayness; smileless, somber, worn-out, the sparkling color long faded from her eyes, the red drained from her cheeks and lips, she recoils from the young child.

> When Dorothy . . . first came to her, Aunt Em had been so startled by the child's laughter that she would scream and press her hand upon her heart whenever Dorothy's merry voice reached her ears; and she still looked at the little girl with wonder that she could find anything to laugh at.[2]

Having lost her own vitality during years of unremitting hardship on the farm, Aunt Em does not respond to Dorothy's innate joyfulness. Covered by a shroud of gloom that separates her from everything and everyone, weighted down and absorbed by her own melancholia, Aunt Em is unable to recognize, appreciate, take pleasure in, mirror, and affirm her growing child.

In order to thrive, Dorothy must separate from the unresponsive Aunt Em. Hence, her healing journey takes her "somewhere over the rainbow," where she receives the maternal gifts of nurturance and empathy from sources more abundant than her own poor Aunt Em. Like Dorothy, survivors of emotionally impoverished homes are forced to be scavengers, to find bits and pieces of life's essentials in all manner of places and, through their cleverness and persistence, accumulate enough to live by. In the magical Land of Oz Dorothy, blessed by the motherspirit of the good Witch of the North, faces great challenges, develops her character, and becomes a model of strength and courage—a beloved and timeless heroine.

Dorothy's separation from Aunt Em begins when a cyclone carries the Gale house along with the little girl and her dog, Toto, far from Kansas and the familiar to a strange and distant place. At first, Dorothy (like any other girl who leaves mother behind) is very frightened that she will be dashed to pieces meeting the unknown. When the cyclone sets her down, however, she discovers that she is in a country of marvelous beauty.

> There were lovely patches of greensward all about, with stately trees bearing rich and luscious fruits. Banks of gorgeous flowers were on every hand, and birds with rare and brilliant plumage sang and fluttered in the trees and bushes. A little way off was a small brook, rushing and sparkling along between green banks, and murmuring in

a voice very grateful to a little girl who had lived so long on the dry, gray prairies.[3]

Looking over her wonderous new surroundings, Dorothy realizes that Aunt Em's gray realm does not represent the whole world, which is, in fact, full of color and riches. But she is not yet ready to receive these gifts. Indeed, Dorothy wishes to return to the emotionally barren woman and the parched Kansas prairies immediately. Like most of us, the young girl is drawn to the familiar, even when it has proven to be unkind, and is fearful of the new, even when it offers possibilities of well-being. As Dorothy expresses, "No matter how dreary and gray our homes are, we people of flesh and blood would rather live there than in any other country, be it ever so beautiful."[4]

Fortunately the good Witch of the North impedes her retreat. Much like a helpful psychotherapist or other enhancing mother figure, the good Witch prepares Dorothy for the long and arduous journey on the yellow brick road that will transform her into a self-confident, resilient, and powerful person. Only after the girl has strengthened her character will she be able to return to the less-than-happy family she left behind and make the best of an imperfect situation.

In great part, Dorothy's journey entails creating a good inner mother. She is required to destroy the bad inner mother (represented by the wicked witches of the east and west), who holds her back and pulls her down, and to take in the good inner mother (represented by the beneficent witches of the north and south), who affirms, protects, nurtures, soothes, lets go, and empowers. Although the representation of mothers as witches may strike some as extreme and unfair, I should like to point out that in the child's mind there are strong similarities in that both mothers and witches are magical figures who, by virtue of their perceived power, can do anything.

Like other compliant females, Dorothy at first resists the tasks before her. Indeed, after the good Witch of the North tells Dorothy that her house landed on the wicked Witch of the East and killed her, the little girl is beside herself with guilt. "Oh, dear! oh, dear! . . . What ever shall we do?" she wails.[5] Her female mentor wisely assures her that there is nothing to do, that it was necessary to deliver a blow to or, literally, "land on" the bad witch—in this case, the archetypal destroyer mother. But "killing" (more accurately, raging at) the bad Witch of the East is only a first step. Dorothy's healing cannot be complete until she develops as a person.[6] And the good Witch—like the empowering mother—pushes her in this direction.

> "How can I get there?" asked Dorothy.
> "You must walk. It is a long journey, through a country that is sometimes pleasant and sometimes dark and terrible. . . ."
> "Won't you go with me?" pleaded the girl, who had begun to look upon the little old woman as her only friend.
> "No, I cannot do that," she replied; "but I will give you my kiss, and no one will dare injure a person who has been kissed by the Witch of the North."[7]

The good Witch first blesses Dorothy with her kiss, which leaves a permanent, round, shining imprint on the little girl's forehead. For Dorothy (as for every child), the motherkiss tenderly communicates the message, "Remember that you are loved and cared for—always." It is this message—at once gentle and powerful—that soothes and encourages during periods of adversity.

Then the good Witch presents Dorothy with the pair of magical silver shoes that the wicked Witch had worn. Both the color silver and the shoes have special meanings.[8] Silver is associated with the moon, whose changing shape suggests the transformations that Dorothy—and all changing, growing women—experience. Shoes, which stand under us, signify *under standing*: comprehension, knowledge, discernment, and also sympathy for others—the means toward humane, full living.[9] Shoes also allow us to move on, to journey across rough land and to venture far from home: They are the fittings of our autonomy.

Blessed with the motherkiss and empowered with the silver shoes, Dorothy begins her trek on the yellow brick road. As she takes her leave, the good Witch of the North points Dorothy in the direction of the Great Wizard of Oz, who resides in the City of Emeralds, suggesting that he may be able to help her return to Kansas. Like unpossessive mothers who encourage their daughters to bond with father, the good Witch advises Dorothy not to be afraid of the Wizard but to tell him her story and ask for his help. And, like many other little girls, Dorothy attributes superhuman powers to the Wizard, whom she idealizes as the perfect father who, by virtue of his absolute strength and power, can do anything, be anything.

As Dorothy embarks on the yellow brick road in search of the great Wizard, she befriends a brainless Scarecrow, a heartless Tin Woodman, and a cowardly Lion. More than Dorothy's loyal companions and delightful characters in their own right, they represent parts of her growing, changing self. As is true for each of us, in order for Dorothy to realize her full potential, she needs to use her intelligence, open her heart, and muster up the courage to take risks.

Just as the Scarecrow "walked straight ahead, and so stepped into the holes and fell at full length on the hard bricks,"[10] in failing to use our brains, we inevitably stumble through life and undermine ourselves. Out of habit and without consciousness, we smart people can act very stupidly and sabotage our happiness. On the other hand, by using our brains—that is, by acting with awareness—we have a much better chance of going where we want to go. Similarly, without heart—empathy, generosity, and tender feelings for others—we, like the love-starved Tin Woodman, are ultimately deprived of happiness. Giving and receiving love is what makes us whole. And, as the Lion sums up, "Life is simply unbearable without a bit of courage."[11]

But how does one get that courage? Despite the best intentions, people who have been neglected, misunderstood, or abused in their original families cannot simply will themselves to be suddenly open and courageous. Over the years, they have typically learned to protect themselves against further hurt by closing themselves off and by compulsively repeating unhealthy, albeit familiar, patterns of living, habits they are not likely to give up easily.

For emotionally wounded people, mental health—thinking in original ways, welcoming intimate relationships, and trying new behaviors when old ones no longer work well—is achieved only gradually and most often with the help of others. This is why psychotherapy with an empathic counselor or participation in a support group is healing. No wonder, then, that as Dorothy makes her long journey, she is aided by nurturing, kindly characters.

Even before she sets out on the yellow brick road that will take her to the City of Emeralds, Dorothy encounters the generous and gentle Munchkins. In their land, fields are not parched but overflow with grains and vegetables, and branches are heavy with hanging fruit. Moreover, unlike the somber parents she left behind in Kansas, the Munchkins are happy men and women who shower the girl with their sweet laughter and song—those priceless parental gifts of joyful love. And unlike the unresponsive Aunt Em and Uncle Henry, they mirror her feelings. For example, when out of homesickness, Dorothy begins to sob, "the kind-hearted Munchkins immediately took out their handkerchiefs and began to weep also."[12]

However, although the Munchkins are wonderfully generous, affirming, and mirroring, they—miniature-sized and almost toylike—are not developed enough to provide Dorothy with all that she requires. Just as human daughters need more from their parents than nurturance and mirroring, Dorothy, if she is to realize her full growth, cannot be satisfied with what the Munchkins offer. Hence, after filling herself up with their nourishment, she must part from them and take from other sources what she needs in order to grow.

On the road to the City of Emeralds, Dorothy and her

companions (or parts of herself) encounter many other creatures, who help, challenge, and also teach them important lessons. For example, a stork—after being assured that she will not be forced to carry a burden that would drag her down—lifts the lightweight Scarecrow from the river where he is stranded and carries him to safe ground. What the stork teaches Dorothy and mortal women as well is that in caring for others, we must still take care of our needs and recognize our limitations—that we must not allow others to drag us down.

Later, hundreds of field mice pull the cowardly Lion away from a deadly meadow of poppies. As he remarks, "I have always thought myself very big and terrible; yet . . . such small animals as mice have saved my life. How strange it all is!"[13] In our individualistic society, which emphasizes autonomy and self-sufficiency, we are apt to deny that we humans are in fact dependent on small kindnesses from others; a little bit of empathy, a thoughtful word, a pat on the back—like the little mice who save the cowardly Lion— can have important effects. Moreover, we commonly fail to acknowledge that the healthiest among us are willing to expose our vulnerability by making our emotional needs known instead of hiding them behind a stiff upper lip. The mice teach the wisdom of asking for help from time to time instead of always insisting we have everything under control.

In addition to being helped by others, Dorothy learns to nurture and soothe, or *mother*, herself. For example, when the Tin Woodman (who, like her other companions, represents an aspect of Dorothy) cries out that he has been groaning for more than a year and that no one has helped him, Dorothy immediately oils his (and her own) hurting parts. In the form of the Scarecrow (another part of herself), whose hands are clumsy as they fill her basket with edible nuts, Dorothy begins to fill herself with the riches of the earth— clumsily at first, as is the case with all unnurtured daughters. Later, like a soothing mother, the Scarecrow covers Dorothy with dry leaves as she lies down to sleep, and these keep her snug and warm.

Besides accepting the kindnesses of others and nurturing herself, Dorothy also learns to care for others. The "magic" of human relationships flows from reciprocity—giving and taking, respecting and being respected, comforting and being comforted, encouraging and being encouraged, affecting and being affected. If we learn only to receive the kindness and indulgence of others, we remain diminished and inferior. However, if we affect others positively, we ourselves are empowered. (This fact accounts for the despair of the "me generation," which has learned to serve only itself rather than itself *and* others.) Dorothy's journey is healing in great part because she takes the opportunity *to give* care and concern: to Toto, to the Queen of the field mice who becomes her friend, to the yellow Winkies whom the wicked Witch of the West enslaved, and, ultimately, to Aunt Em, for whom she has much sympathy and concern despite the woman's inadequacies as a parent.

In the benign environment of empathy, compassion, and concern, Dorothy and her companions realize their full human potentials. The "brainless" Scarecrow, time and time again, uses his cleverness to overcome obstacles along the yellow brick road; the "heartless" Tin Woodman treats others with special kindness and sensitivity; the "cowardly" Lion performs many acts of courage despite his awareness of danger. When, toward the end of the tale, the Wizard of Oz presents the Scarecrow with brains, the Tin Woodman with a heart, and the Lion with courage, he is only recognizing and affirming the attributes that have always been a part of them but, by virtue of their insecurity, had remained hidden.

I am reminded of several of my own clients who, during the course of therapy, discover that despite their childhood deprivations they are not deficient human beings; the qualities they assumed were missing in themselves—intelligence, lovingness, lovableness, and courage—had simply been *unrealized*, and in the presence of an encouraging, empathic,

affirming other—therapist or friend or mentor or love partner—they unfold. As the Wizard wisely explains to the Lion,
"All you need is confidence in yourself."[14]

Of course, Dorothy's healing journey is not smooth; transformations never are. Dorothy, like so many women struggling toward recovery, falls into potentially lethal traps. For
example, just after she and her companions have safely
passed through a dark forest where they overcome many
discouragements, they find themselves in a meadow of brilliant, spicy-scented scarlet poppies. As Dorothy breathes in
the powerful odor of the flowers, she temporarily falls into
a coma. She is seduced by the deadly flowers much the way
other wounded daughters are seduced by mind-altering
drugs or alcohol. These substances create an illusion of well-
being, of inner calm, of oneness with the world, and are a
dangerous substitute for the tranquility more fortunate
daughters have experienced and internalized with the soothing mother of childhood. No wonder that Dorothy succumbs
to the powers of the poisonous poppies and that her friends
the Scarecrow and Tin Woodman must carry her away from
the tainted meadow to save her from death. (I am reminded
of the members of the popular Twelve-Step programs such
as Alcoholics Anonymous who are, figuratively speaking,
carried away from disabling addictions by their "sponsors,"
the recovering men and women who now are helpers and
healers.)

Another time, after Dorothy has succeeded in melting the
wicked Witch of the West and is about to return in triumph
to the Emerald City, she and her companions lose their
bearings in a great field of yellow daisies and buttercups and
for many days get nowhere. Being temporarily lost and confused, however, is natural to the healing process and leads
to new and clearer paths. When we do not become overly
discouraged by setbacks, when we press on despite our confusion, we are bound to make new discoveries.

Had she not lost her way, for example, Dorothy would
not have had reason to discover her powers of leadership
—symbolized by the Golden Cap she wears. With her

Golden Cap, she summons the Winged Monkeys, who used to obey the wicked Witch, brings them under her own control, and directs them to transport her to the Emerald City. An incident from my practice comes to mind. After a long depression, a client of mine who had always bowed to the demands of her imperious mother, stood up to her at last. Full of new confidence, she told me, "I never saw myself as a commanding woman. But I am. I just had to spend some time in this dark place to discover myself. Painful as my depression was, it was necessary and has helped me grow."

As the good Witch of the North promised, Dorothy's journey in the magical Land of Oz is full of delights and terrors. Most terrifying of all is Dorothy's encounter with the wicked Witch of the West, who symbolizes a very destructive mother spirit indeed. The wicked Witch torments Dorothy and her company, commanding various creatures who threaten to mutilate and destroy them. What saves the little girl is the mark of the good Witch's motherkiss, which still shines on Dorothy's forehead. The motherkiss provides Dorothy with the feeling that she is lovable and therefore precious and worthy. Without it, Dorothy might very well believe that she deserves to be mistreated.

In my practice, I have frequently observed that at the point when a woman realizes that she is lovable and precious and worthy and that she does not deserve abuse—from her mother or anyone else—she takes the necessary action to stop it, to say firmly, "Your behavior toward me is simply unacceptable! I can only be in a relationship with you if you treat me with common decency." As long as she has too little self-respect, however, she tends to put up with indignities.

The Witch's cruel machinations, which Dorothy knows she does not deserve, fuel the girl's righteous indignation, which ultimately sets her free. Interestingly, it is the Witch's attempt to rob Dorothy of her most valuable assets, her understanding and her autonomy (which are represented by the Silver Shoes), that precipitates Dorothy's necessary confrontation with her.

"You are a wicked creature!" cried Dorothy. "You have no right to take my shoe from me."

"I shall keep it just the same," said the Witch, laughing at her, "and some day I shall get the other one from you, too."

This made Dorothy so very angry that she picked up the bucket of water that stood near and dashed it over the Witch, wetting her from head to foot.

Instantly the wicked woman gave a loud cry of fear and then, as Dorothy looked at her in wonder, the Witch began to shrink and fall away.

"See what you have done!" she screamed. "In a minute I shall melt away."[15]

Dorothy is set free because she is no longer cowed by the mother's abusive power. She is instead justifiably outraged and determined to put an end to it. Let us remember that to understand is *not always* to forgive and forget. When daughters come to understand that the mother in whom they had vested their child's trust has, instead of treating them tenderly, been cruel, they have a right to their intense anger at her; they even have a right to withhold forgiveness. I have watched women who as children were maltreated break out of lifelong depressions as they express and I affirm their right to be outraged at the mother who failed them so miserably. Previously denied the right to direct their anger against their mother, they had instead turned it against themselves, where it festered.

Paradoxically, after permitting herself the right to rage and to confront her mother's injustices, the daughter often finds it easier to empathize with her—to understand, although not necessarily excuse, her behavior. As we will see in Chapter 9, articulation of one's angry feelings can have the effect of *melting* them, in which case tolerance of the mother's past injustices and a nonexploitative mother-daughter relationship in the present do become possible.

To be sure, becoming angry at mother for her injustices and losing the ideal of the beneficent mother are painful.

Some daughters compensate by idealizing father—creating, as Dorothy does, the illusion of the all-powerful male parent. Placing all her trust in the wizardry of Oz, Dorothy believes only he can grant her most important wish: transporting her to Kansas and to Aunt Em. And although Oz impresses Dorothy with his magic by appearing in various guises, both beautiful and scary, in the end, he necessarily disappoints her unreasonable expectations of him, and she must consequently come to terms with his ordinariness.

> Oz had not kept the promise he made her, but he had done his best, so she forgave him. As he said, he was a good man, even if he was a bad Wizard.[16]

Identifying with an idealized parent helps every young child build self-esteem; believing the parent to be strong and wonderful allows her to believe that she is strong and wonderful; believing the parent to be all-powerful allows her to feel safe in a not-too-safe world. As each of us grows up, however, we must give up at least some of our illusions. One of the marks of full adulthood is the capacity to see one's parents not as godlike or monstrous but rather as human—that is, imperfect and fallible. Accomplishing this, we spare ourselves continual disappointment in them, and we are ready for an adult-to-adult friendship.

Soon after discovering and accepting the Wizard's ordinariness, Dorothy and her three companions set out to meet Glinda, the good Witch of the South, who is the archetypal good mother—nurturing and protective but also growth-enhancing and vibrant, vital and full of color.

> She was both beautiful and young to their eyes. Her hair was a rich red in color and fell in flowing ringlets over her shoulders. Her dress was pure white; but her eyes were blue, and they looked kindly upon the little girl. . . .

Glinda leaned forward and kissed the sweet, upturned face of the loving little girl.

"Bless your heart," she said, "I am sure I can tell you of a way to get back to Kansas."[17]

Glinda then tells Dorothy that her Silver Shoes, which are the symbol of understanding, have wonderful powers and can take her anyplace in the world, including Kansas. By addressing the powers of the Silver Shoes, Glinda—the good inner mother—articulates the essential moral of Baum's tale: The power to make our wishes come true resides within us, not outside of us. Wizards and other self-appointed gurus cannot rescue us, but neither can bad Witch/mothers destroy us.

When, at Glinda's urging, Dorothy closes her eyes, claps the heels of her shoes together three times, and calls out, "Take me home to Aunt Em!" she is much changed from the little girl we meet at the beginning of the tale. In the course of her journey, she has accepted the kindnesses of others and been herself kind to others; she has encountered the Wizard-father, discovered him to be an ordinary man, and forgiven him for his ordinariness; she has confronted and set herself free from the destructive mother, who is controlling and abusive, and has internalized the positive mother, who protects, nurtures, affirms, soothes, empowers, and lets go. Having made use of her brains and her heart, and having mustered up much courage, she has taken from the plentiful universe what she requires in order to grow and thrive. Because she has become a person in her own right, Dorothy can return to Aunt Em and cope with a difficult home situation. Aunt Em is not all a mother should be, but unless she is a cruel person, every mother to her daughter is still "home sweet home."

L. Frank Baum's *The Wizard of Oz* is richer from a psychological perspective than the movie version. One of the sequences included only in the book that is particularly illuminating describes an adventure in "The Dainty China Country." On the last leg of their journey, just before they meet the good Glinda, Dorothy and her company come to a charming country that is made entirely of china. Here our heroine encounters a beautifully dressed princess who tries to run away from her.

> Dorothy wanted to see more of the Princess, so she ran after her; but the china girl cried out:
> "Don't chase me! don't chase me!"
> She had such a frightened little voice that Dorothy stopped and said,
> "Why not?"
> "Because," answered the princess, also stopping a safe distance away, "If I run I may fall down and break myself."
> "But couldn't you be mended?" asked the girl.
> "Oh, yes; but one is never so pretty after being mended, you know," replied the princess.[18]

For all its charm, Dorothy and her fellow travelers are relieved to leave this country of fragile china people. As the Scarecrow remarks, "I am thankful I am made of straw and cannot be easily damaged."[19] Indeed, in the course of their arduous and marvelous journey, Dorothy, the Scarecrow, the Tin Woodman, and the cowardly Lion have been broken and mended; they have stumbled, tripped, fallen flat on their faces but always gotten back on their feet again. While changing, growing, and struggling may also rob us of an innocent prettiness, they allow us to become resilient and resourceful, which is not a bad trade-off.

# PART III

 *Healings*

What was painful and destructive I have made into
something of my own, changed the sorrow into something vital and accessible.

—Gloria Vanderbilt
*Woman to Woman*

# CHAPTER 6

# *Reparative Relationships*

Love is not deserved, is unmerited—it is simply grace.

—Viktor E. Frankl
*The Doctor and the Soul*

Many years ago, when I first began counseling, I observed my psychiatric supervisor in a session with a chronically depressed patient. Slouched over in her chair, her finely chiseled face set into what had become a permanent scowl, the young woman whispered, "What's the point of living? The world is a nasty place; people are *bad*." Dr. Shapiro leaned toward her, smiled softly, and said, "Funny, but my world is good and the people in it are pretty nice." Although this verbal exchange seemed less than dramatic at the time, its meaning affects me still. As the embittered young woman rightly concluded, people are bad: violent, cruel, greedy, and self-serving. But as the good doctor correctly posited, people are gentle, kind, generous, and loving. To a large degree, our well-being—whether we perceive the world as good or nasty—depends on whom we select as our companions and how we are nurtured in these relationships.

The more fortunate daughters among us are, from the time of our birth, tended by mature and loving parents who appreciate and approve of us. Because the first relationship is a precedent for all others, we fortunate daughters are likely to be attracted to people who, like our parents, enhance us. Moreover, having been filled with the riches of parental love, we will naturally love others. As psychiatrist Irvin Yalom

says so eloquently, "Mature caring flows out of one's richness, not out of one's poverty."[1]

The less fortunate daughters among us, however, are
raised by parents who are inadequate in significant ways.
Sadly, we daughters may be drawn to similarly impoverished
people for the very fact that they are familiar—that they
represent "home." The bitter irony is that those of us who
require a great deal of love and affirmation to compensate
for our deprived childhoods often cultivate relationships
with people who are themselves too wounded to give.

The main purpose of this chapter is to describe human
relationships that are healing and lead to fuller, more satisfying lives. But first I would like to present two case studies
that reveal the traps into which women deprived of adequate
maternal love typically fall. In order for women to freely
choose sustaining relationships, we must become aware of
the kinds of relationship that doom us to unhappiness.

Sara, an appealing woman in her middle twenties, came
to see me about a marriage problem. According to Sara, her
husband, Sam, was emotionally inaccessible and with him
she felt lonely and neglected. What became clear to me after
a few sessions was that Sara's relationship with Sam was
remarkably similar to the one she had with her mother years
before.

When I was little, I remember trying to make my mother
take an interest in me. I was very bubbly. Always on. I
would sing for her, invent and act out funny little skits
that I thought might make her laugh. But despite my best
efforts, my mother didn't seem to want to be bothered by
me. She was mostly distracted. She would blow me off.

We used to move a lot because of my mother's work as
an actress. We were always packing up to go somewhere
else. I remember worrying that she would one day forget

that I was there and leave me behind in a railroad station or bus depot, the way one might inadvertently leave behind a piece of luggage.

Sara met Sam while they were still in high school. She was immediately drawn to the shy, handsome boy with the sad hazel eyes. After she learned about his troubled childhood from a mutual friend, Sara knew that she wanted to spend her life with him—to undo with loving kindness the emotional damage his mother and father, who had sexually abused him, had caused. Moreover, having been hurt as a child, Sara—like so many other wounded women—had always been attracted to wounded men, for whom she had a special sympathy. For his part, Sam did not reject Sara's romantic overtures, although he seemed more a passive observer of their relationship than an active partner.

Married when they were both twenty, Sara and Sam seemed quite happy during the first year. Busy fixing up their home, delighted by the novelty of shopping for groceries and preparing gourmet meals for her new husband, Sara did not demand much of Sam; she was content just to be around him when he came home from work, plopped in front of the TV for the evening, or settled behind the newspaper. But after she became pregnant, Sara's needs for her husband's nurturance and reassurances began to emerge. She wanted to be close in a new way—to snuggle on the couch, to talk about their relationship, to find out his opinions, to make plans for the baby. However, Sara's reasonable requests for intimacy overwhelmed Sam. Increasingly, he drew away from her. The night that Sara went into labor, Sam was out of town on business and could not be reached.

Neglected by Sam, Sara felt insignificant; indeed, in his presence, she experienced herself as hardly there. Housework and baby care being not enough to sustain her, her desperation for emotional contact, with a partner who consistently ignored her, made her frantic. For example, in order to win Sam's attention, she would follow him from room to room, compulsively asking him questions while he tended to ignore her or answer only mechanically. Or, increasingly frustrated by his inattention, she would sometimes scream abuses at him, which momentarily at least precipitated a reaction but ultimately left her feeling like a witch. When Sam was at work, Sara frequently suffered from bouts of anxious paranoia: "Is he having an affair with someone at work?" she wondered. Because she was getting no attention from Sam, she wondered if he was giving his love to someone else.

Sara insisted that, above all else, she desired a warm, loving family life. Yet, as I pointed out, she had chosen as marriage partner a man who would not be intimate. Introverted and inexpressive, Sam found human interactions painful—even those with his lovely wife. Most frustrating to Sara, he denied there were any problems with their marriage. Though to placate Sara he had come to three counseling sessions with her, he squirmed in his chair, glanced furtively at his watch, and, like a trapped animal who is suddenly freed, bolted from the consulting room as soon as I announced that our time was up.

This poor man, the victim of unspeakably cruel parents, had long ago developed a protective shell that grew so hard and thick none could penetrate it. And with Sam, Sara felt unconnected, unnoticed, unimportant—*just as she had felt with her mother*. Unwittingly, Sara had recreated in her adult life the emotionally cold, unhealthy milieu of her childhood.


Deirdre, a bright, energetic woman in her late thirties, entered therapy because, despite her best efforts, she was unable to cultivate satisfying friendships. She was particularly distressed about a destructive relationship with a womanfriend, one that mimicked her own destructive relationship with her mother.

When I asked Deirdre to tell me about her mother, she described her as dour and critical—the "world champion of the backhanded compliment."

Whatever my mother gave me with her right hand, she was sure to take away with her left: "For the life of me, Deirdre, I can't understand how a girl with brains in her head can make such a mess of her life"; or "I really thought you looked attractive *before* you had your hair cut so short"; or "You should thank your lucky stars that a smart, nice fellow like Joey is interested in someone like *you*"; or "My, what a great wardrobe you have! How are you ever able to spend so much money on yourself without feeling guilty?"

As Deirdre explained, "With Mother, I always felt that if I hadn't done what I just did, I might have been a fine person." According to Deirdre, mother was especially disapproving after Deirdre divorced her husband, Joey. ("You could have had a nice family, but for some reason you have to bring misery upon yourself and my poor grandkids!")

Two years after her divorce and the continuing condemnations from mother, Deirdre decided to cut ties with her. However, just as she freed herself from this undermining relationship, she began a friendship with a woman who resembled her mother. Like Deirdre's mother, Elizabeth was adept at pointing out Deirdre's "shortcomings."

Elizabeth is my Jiminy Cricket. She is my conscience, reminding me of my duties as an upstanding citizen or as a good mother—duties that I never seem to live up to: "Now that you're dating, Deirdre, you probably have your mind on other things, but are you aware that you missed a really important PTA meeting last night?" or "I thought I'd ask your daughter over to bake some brownies with me and my kids. I know she doesn't get a chance to bake with you, what with your working and all, and I just feel so bad that she's missing out on a good family life."

As Deirdre explained, after practically every encounter with Elizabeth, Deirdre felt diminished, guilty, and miserable: "For instance, even though I know my children are happy and well-adjusted, Elizabeth makes me feel I'm a terrible mother." Yet Deirdre did not try to put a stop to Elizabeth's subtle abuses, but returned to her time and again for more punishment, which Elizabeth doled out effortlessly. As she explained, "It is true that I am worse off for my 'friendship' with Elizabeth, but she's the only person I know with whom I really feel comfortable; she's like family."

For Deirdre, trusting and feeling comfortable and familiar with Elizabeth were easy because Elizabeth confirmed mother's poor opinions of her. As novelist and diarist Anaïs Nin once wrote, "You [retain] as upon a delicate retina, your mother's image of you, as the first and only authentic one, her judgments of your acts."[2]

As I suggested earlier, we seek and trust what is known to us, so that, like Sara and Deirdre, we may automatically choose companions who resemble our parents. To be sure, these resemblances are not always obvious. I am currently counseling a woman who set out to marry a man who would be nothing like her despised father. Yet, although father and husband are different in appearance and demeanor—the former plays the bumbler and the fool, the latter the "macho man"—both are excessively needy and dependent. Just as my client felt drained throughout her childhood by her father's unreasonable demands, she is swallowed up by a husband who insists that she wait on him hand and foot.

I have also counseled couples who are determined to relate to each other much differently than their parents related to them; yet they manage to undermine themselves. For example, one client who complains that his mother constantly nagged him nevertheless provokes his wife—ordinarily an undemanding, easy-going woman—to act just like her. Then he growls, "Women are all shrews!" There is a wise saying that the marriage bed holds not two but six—the wedded couple, his parents, and hers.

We repeat patterns of relationship because the repetitions allow us to feel comfortable, to remain on familiar turf. In one way, we are all biased experimental scientists. We are

continually looking for evidence that confirms what we believe to be true. Hence, if our mothers disapproved of us,
we may gravitate toward those who think little of us and
thereby confirm what she and we have "known" all along—
that we are pretty worthless—or stupid or ugly or lazy or
crazy or mean or selfish. Of course, we do not consciously
set out to form ties with hurtful people. As one of my clients
observed, "I say that I want to be with kind and gentle men,
but I tend to end up with angry ones who abuse me, just
as my mother did. There seems to be some weird sort of
chemistry that draws them to me and me to them."

We also repeat childhood relationships because we want
to correct what went wrong with them in the first place: We
want a second chance. For example, if we were denied motherlove as children, we may throughout our adulthoods continue to seek such love from mother or, more commonly,
from others who represent her; and we work hard—oh, so
hard—*to earn* the maternal approval that we could never take
for granted. Again, we do not consciously decide to relive
our past but rather, without being fully aware, fall into such
repetitions. Sara and Deirdre, for example, were drawn to
people who were stand-ins for the mothers from whom they
craved affirmation. Not surprisingly, Sara's and Deirdre's
efforts to gain love from Sam and Elizabeth failed. One cannot expect loving-kindness from those poor souls who lack
the capacity to give. A client of mine put it well: "A starving
puppy isn't going to be nourished if it pulls at empty teats."

The wish to fix what went wrong during childhood is not
only fueled by our self-interest. As much as we want a
second chance to be loved, we also want our mothers to
have a second chance to love us and to be good people. If
they were weak—or harsh or withholding or sick—we try
to help them or those who represent them become strong—
or gentle or giving or healthy. Sara, for example, always
sensed that her mother's distraction and apparent lack of
concern for her masked a profound sadness. Despite all her
forced cheeriness, however, Sara the child failed to soothe

her mother's wounded spirit. By setting out to love and thereby heal Sam—the stand-in for Sara's mother—Sara was indirectly trying to heal her mother.

The grown child's unconscious desire to make the deficient parent whole is illuminated in Robert Zerneckis's fanciful and wonderful *Back to the Future*. In this film, the adolescent son of a weak, bumbling father travels back in time to the father's own youth, befriends him, and encourages him to be strong. For example, the son successfully persuades his new friend (really his father) to stand up to the school bully, which he never did in reality, thereby helping him to become the courageous, powerful man he was meant to be: the good father of every boy's dreams. Sadly, although everything is possible in the movies, real life is more restrictive. We cannot redo our pasts to change our futures; we cannot remake our parents.

As a psychotherapist, I have learned that every individual strives toward growth and well-being and that the psyche is endlessly inventive in trying to heal itself. However, sometimes the strategies employed by the psyche are faulty and, instead of healing, they make matters worse. Repeating compulsively the disabling relationships of childhood in an effort to redo them—the trap that countless wounded women fall into—is one example of a faulty strategy. As Judith Viorst writes in *Necessary Losses*:

> [The repetition compulsion] impels us to do again and again what we have done before, to attempt to restore an earlier state of being. It impels us to transfer the past—our ancient longings, our defenses against those longings—onto the present.
>
> Thus whom we love and how we love are revivals—unconscious revivals—of early experience, even when revivals bring us pain. And . . . we will act out the same old tragedies unless awareness and insight intervene.[3]

It is not easy to break free from our compulsions.[4] Even Dorothy, the heroine of Oz, wants to cling to the familiar—

gray and dreary as it is. But eventually, with the aid of her Silver Shoes (the symbol of transformation and self-understanding) and the encouragement of the good Witch of the North, she relinquishes the comfort of the familiar and ventures forth into the foreign Land of Oz, where she observes that the sun shines brightly, birds sing sweetly, and fields are rich with grains and vegetables. Indeed, as she proceeds on her healing journey, Dorothy sees that the world is not only dreary gray but also various as the colors of a rainbow. She is drawn to good witches; she discovers people who, unlike the depressed Aunt Em, do not recoil from her child's laughter and merry voice but frolic with her; and she joins with those who do not destroy her spirit but instead enhance it.

Happily, I have also watched real women break free from depressing relationships. Instead of repeatedly and compulsively drawing close to those who make them miserable (or provoking others to treat them miserably), they form vital, growth-enhancing ties and, in so doing, create for themselves a world that is abundant and good.

But how do we move away from destructive relationships toward constructive ones? First, we must become aware when we are repeating patterns; we must put on our Silver Shoes to gain new self-understanding. It is common for a client to say, "Until recently, I had no idea that there was a pattern to my relationships. I was not aware that I was choosing people who reminded me of my first family or that I was acting out of habit; it didn't *feel* as if I was repeating anything! But now I am beginning to see differently."

Moreover, we must accept that forming attachments with those who relentlessly tear at or pull us down can come to no good. Quite wisely, Dorothy does not try to win love from the wicked Witch of the West, nor does she try to rehabilitate her, nor does she gravitate toward others who remind her of the Witch's cruelty. Similarly, we must free ourselves from, rather than seek out, those people who consistently bring us misery. One of my Buddhist clients explains that in her religion the word "trust" does not mean a naive belief in others' goodness and integrity; rather it refers to an accurate understanding of the world as it is. Hence, one trusts that a rock is hard and that banging against it will cause injury; one trusts that the ocean water is cold and that submerging oneself in it will be chilling; *and one trusts that certain people are malicious or exploitative or emotionally unavailable and that keeping company with them will cause much misery.*

Trusting that Sam was not willing to be in an intimate relationship, Sara was eventually able to leave him. With the help of therapy, she became aware of having repeated with her husband the disabling relationship that she had suffered with her mother. Moreover, she decided not to repeat her mistake again but to form more rewarding friendships. To this end, Sara joined a support group in which she cultivated ties with warm and generous people. As one would expect, however, at first Sara felt uneasy with her new friends. For example, unused to others' concern for her, she felt awkward at being the focus of attention or even receiving a compliment. One of my tasks as Sara's therapist was to help her identify and become comfortable with enhancing interactions between people. She had been so used to negative interactions that she experienced them as normal. Now she had to learn new standards of human behavior. As Sara said toward the end of her treatment:

> I still blush when people pay attention to me, but I'm learning to accept these attentions more gracefully. I say to myself, "What I had before was 'bad normal' and this is 'good normal.' "

Turning toward basically caring, loving, affirming people does not, however, ensure satisfying relationships. In order to be in such relationships, one must also be able to care for, love, and affirm the other. Relationship is, after all, a mutual process. It is my experience that many people who were neglected or exploited as children are not ready to love freely and generously. Because they do not feel full themselves, selfless love and friendship cannot yet flow from them. So desperate for the motherlove they missed and continue to crave, they turn to relationships primarily to be mirrored and adored and filled up by another. Emotionally starved, they use their partners to feed their egos but are unable to be truly supportive and loving toward their partners. A former client of mine who flitted from one romantic love to another once said, "All a man—any man—needs to do is love *me*—tell me I'm beautiful and wonderful—and I am his." As psychoanalyst Erich Fromm points out, "Infantile love follows the principle 'I love because I am loved.' Mature love follows the principle: 'I am loved because I love.' Immature love says, 'I love you because I need you.' Mature love says, 'I need you because I love you.' "[5]

If one is to form relationships that bring out the best in each partner, one must be whole—or at least moving toward wholeness. Recalling Yalom's words, we see that "Mature caring flows out of one's richness, not out of one's poverty." What is most heartening about our culture is that increasing numbers of people have the courage to expose their wounds and the determination to heal them. For many, psychotherapy is the yellow brick road that leads to inner wholeness and the psychotherapist the trusted companion on this journey.

It is most important to understand, however, that the relationship between therapist and client is not a *normal* but rather a *reparative* one. At its best, the therapeutic relationship compensates for the deprivations suffered in childhood and prepares the client for satisfying human encounters in the real world. "Real" relationships require mutual concern and attention; therapeutic relationships are one-sided. In the therapeutic relationship, the therapist exists solely for the well-being of the client. His or her purposes are to give, not to take; to nurture, not to be nurtured; to understand, not to be understood; to affirm, not to be affirmed. Other than monetary payment—fees for service—and the client's attendance at sessions, the effective therapist asks for no return.

Allow me a short digression. When Jenny, a friend of mine who as a child had been sexually molested by both grandfathers, read the first draft of this chapter, she became both sad and angry: "You are writing how healing therapy is and how benevolent therapists are. That wasn't my experience at all. Because my first therapist knew that I had already been sexually abused as a child, he was all too ready to follow suit and seduce me—and I was only twelve years old then!" Jenny went on to tell me that never having known affection from her parents, she had at first welcomed the therapist's physical attentions—invitations to sit on his lap and "fatherly" caresses—which then gradually became sexualized: "How easy it is for the unhugged little girl—so hungry for parental affection—to allow a trusted adult to exploit her. How confusing for the unsuspecting child when touch, at first gentle and kindly, becomes violating."

Unfortunately, we cannot assume that all therapists are scrupulous. Some—consciously or unconsciously—use their clients for their own purposes.[6] Certainly, therapists embrace different philosophies and employ various techniques, but what clients need to know absolutely is that *the therapist who pursues with his or her client a two-sided relationship in the form of friendship or love or sex always undoes the potential good of psychotherapy and, in many cases, causes great harm.* Sadly, those clients who as children or teenagers had been exploited—those clients who are most fragile and vulnerable—are the ones likely to be similarly exploited by therapists: another example of the tendency toward repetition.

Knowing about Jenny's destructive experiences in therapy and aware that many male and female clients have had similar ones, I nevertheless continue to believe that most therapists are ethical and, as the following vignette illustrates, that they can help clients become fuller, more self-respecting human beings.

Krista, a former client of mine, had been used either sexually or emotionally by virtually every significant person in her life. Aware that I was writing a book about adult daughters, Krista offered, during one of her early sessions, to share anecdotes about her own relationship to her emotionally abusive mother *that would be useful to me*. When I explained that our therapy hour was meant to be useful to her, not to me, and that I could not in all good conscience accept her offer, Krista looked incredulous. After a long silence, she began to weep quietly. Having always believed that her purpose on this earth was only to serve others, she was at first taken aback, then deeply moved, by my refusal.

As therapy continued, Krista became more comfortable receiving the nurture—attention to *her* needs, interest in *her* well-being—I provided. She learned firsthand how it feels to be valued, rather than used, and heard for the first time positive maternal messages: "Krista, you are a fine and worthy and lovable young woman. What you say and do is of interest to me." Over time, she took in—or internalized—my affirmations and began to treat herself with some care. For example, she no longer ran herself ragged serving others. Whereas she had typically skipped lunch when extra work was piled on her desk, she began to insist on a noon break, saying, "I am getting it into my head finally that I deserve to eat a sandwich or have a yogurt, even if it is an inconvenience to my boss."

At the conclusion of therapy, Krista was by no means ready to take on the world. But neither was she self-abusing. In small ways, she had learned to treat herself kindly—to become a good mother to herself. At our last session, Krista expressed appreciation for the undivided attention I had shown her. Having once been cared for unselfishly, she felt somehow better about herself and reasonably sure that she would never again tolerate others' exploitation. Certainly, the effective therapist cannot undo the abuses of the real mother of childhood. But she can be like the good fairy in *The Sleeping Beauty*, who does not cancel the curse of the thirteenth and vengeful fairy but transforms it with her blessing.

For women who have come to believe that unless they feel, think, and behave in acceptable ways, they will be deserted or otherwise punished, the therapist's unqualified acceptance is crucial. When I think back on the time that I was in therapy, I remember—and with absolute clarity—my therapist's expression of care and kindness whenever I dared reveal my dark, ignoble sides. To confide sexual longings, illicit thoughts, shameful acts, jealousies, failures, fears, vanities, and anger (even at her) without threat of abandonment or recrimination was wonderfully affirming. Because Katharine accepted all parts of me, I slowly began to do the same.

In a similar vein, to share my dark secrets without fear of overwhelming Katharine was a great relief. Like many women I have counseled, I had as a small child come to believe that expressing my pain would irreparably hurt my mother, and so I had always kept it to myself. In fact, I had learned to shut down most of my feelings by becoming a very, very quiet girl. One of my aunts even nicknamed me "Squeaky" because, as she said, "You have the tiniest voice, Evi, just like the squeak of a little mouse." Because I felt safe with Katharine, I discovered my lost voice and learned that my words were not dangerous. I also learned that, in my childish grandiosity, I had overestimated my powers and that my thoughts, feelings, and truths would not *devastate* Katharine (or anyone else, mother included).

Psychoanalyst Alice Miller once said: In a good therapy, a "silent child" evolves into a "talking child"; in a good therapy, the patient finds words for her pain. Not surprisingly, Deirdre, the client whom I described earlier, once told me that the most valuable aspect of our therapy was that I did not censor, trivialize, minimize, or mistrust her words.

I am a product of the "Bambi" school of thought: "If you can't say anything nice, don't say anything at all." So I was afraid that when I told you how angry I was at my mother for hurting me, you would tell me that I wasn't being nice: *that I shouldn't blame her.* But you didn't do that at all. You said, "Deirdre, of course you are right to feel hurt and angry. Your mother's remarks are terribly unkind." What a relief I felt.

It is marvelously freeing for us women to be able to speak, knowing that another listens to us and hears us. When just one trusted soul believes in us, we begin to believe in ourselves—to honor our ideas, feelings, thoughts, sensations, and intuitions. And because we are no longer afraid or ashamed to be who we are, we become whole. No one, to my knowledge, has expressed this sentiment more touchingly than poet, novelist, and critic Gertrude Stein.

You write a book [and while you write it] you are ashamed for everyone must think you are a silly or crazy one and yet you write it and you are ashamed, you know you will be laughed at or pitied by everyone and you have a queer feeling and you are not very certain and you go on writing. Then someone says yes to it, to something you are liking, or doing or making and then never again can you have completely such a feeling of being afraid and ashamed that you had then when you were writing or liking the thing and not anyone had said yes about the thing.[7]

In my therapy, Katharine said Yes!—to the things I was feeling, doing, creating—many times over. Although other people in my life validate me, Katharine's affirmations had a special power because I idealized her. It is true that idealizing another gets in the way of everyday relationships, but let us remember that the relationship with a therapist is not a normal, real-life one. Indeed, an idealized view of the therapist can be beneficial as long as the therapist does not abuse it to gratify his or her own needs as, for example, my friend's seductive therapist did.

Because I believed in Katharine's superiority, I accepted her affirmations; because I invested her with a certain power, she was better able to enpower me. In *The Wizard of Oz*, the regal and resplendent Glinda the Good, perched on her throne of rubies, informs Dorothy of her innate ability to go anywhere she likes. It is reasonable to assume that because Glinda is perceived as "larger-than-life," Dorothy believes her without question; basking in her glow, Dorothy also glows. To be sure, the idealized Glinda does encourage Dorothy to return to her ordinary, flesh-and-blood mother, Aunt Em—just as the idealized therapist encourages her clients to develop down-to-earth relationships with others.

Idealized relationships are lovely, but they are not lasting; only those relationships in which each person is perceived realistically can endure. The relationship between therapist and client necessarily comes to an end. Just like the caretaking early mother, the effective therapist works herself out of a job. Nevertheless, although the face-to-face encounters between therapist and client end, the spirit of the therapist does not desert the client. In Irwin Yalom's words,

> No matter that the patient's relationship to the therapist is "temporary," the *experience* of intimacy is permanent. It can never be taken away. It exists in one's inner world as a permanent reference point: a reminder of one's potential for intimacy. The discovery of self that ensues as a result of intimacy is also permanent.[8]

Although psychotherapy is a road frequently traveled, it is not the only route toward wholeness, and the relationship between client and therapist is not the only reparative one. I have known several women, for example, who as youngsters were helped immeasurably by the attentions of a kind teacher, a clergyman, a family member, a mentor, a nanny, or even the parent of a friend. Even after these helpful people no longer played an active role, memories of them—of their affirmations, approving glances, and enabling words—effected very positive changes. As a client once said, "I believed that I had never been valued, but then I remembered an old neighbor from my childhood—how she would smile at me and make a fuss over my good school grades. Remembering her, I feel less embittered about my life. Knowing that someone did care about me makes a big difference. It tells me that I was a lovable little girl after all." Certainly, mother is the most significant presence in a child's life, but she is not the only influence. Women who as children were not adequately tended by their mothers are often helped as they remember—and honor—the nurturing "others" who visited their childhoods.[9]

One of the most beautiful examples of the enduring effects that a caring adult can have appears in Reynolds Price's novel *Kate Vaiden*. In the following excerpt, we see how Kate, whose parents die violently when she is eleven, is sustained throughout her life by the thoughtful acts of a beloved teacher.

My teacher was of course an old maid, Miss Limer; but I thought she looked like Loretta Young, and I worshipped her tracks. I'd memorized her clothes and could prophesy the day she'd wear which dress. Right to this minute I can smell her rich hair that was as dark as good loam. When [she was told about the violent deaths of Kate's parents] . . . she didn't say a word but took her own stationery (blue with rough edges) and wrote a short letter in her beautiful hand.

*To Whom It May Concern:*
*Kate Vaiden has been an excellent student this entire year in the whole fifth grade. She excels in reading, drawing, and music. She is also kind to her classmates, friends, and appropriate elders. The one small failing is common to her age, a tendency to talk.*
*I commend her to any other teacher's close attention. She is rarely deserving of meticulous care.*
                    *Rosalind Limer, eighteen years as teacher*

She put it in an envelope and then gave it to Swift [a relative]. Then she finally looked at me.

I couldn't help smiling and she stood up and came forward to me, those long legs whispering sweet secrets in her stockings. I could see what she had in her hand but couldn't believe it. All year I'd admired her paperweight, a glass rectangle with a real seahorse inside laid on cotton. I had asked her more than once where she got it; but she never had said, just laughed me off.

When she got to my desk that last day though, she said

"You used to be interested in this; do you think you are still?"

I told her "Yes ma'm."

So she laid it in front of me—the little brown creature facing off to my right through his dry eye-socket. I didn't know whether to touch it or not.

Miss Limer said "That was sent to me by a boy I loved, from the port where he sailed to fight the World War."

The word *love* in her dignified mouth shocked me almost more than the whole last week. But it thrilled me too. She had opened me a tunnel onto some distant light. I believed for the first time I'd be loved again, someday if I lasted.

Swift said "Thank her, Kate." I wished he would blow away.

Miss Limer said "That would be premature." She shot him one of her blistering looks. Then like he really had vanished, she said "You take this from me now and go." She touched me, the first time she'd ever touched a student in my presence.

I cherished the spot, on my left collarbone, till I grew and it faded. And more times than one in the years to come, I'd stare at her seahorse or reread the letter and try to remind myself I should live.[10]

Earlier in this book, I wrote that survivors of emotionally impoverished families are like scavengers: They make do with bits and pieces of human goodness found here and there. As I conclude this chapter on reparative relationships, a particularly touching story comes to mind. It is about one such survivor, a former client—Annie, the daughter of a schizophrenic mother.

Because her illness so incapacitated her, Annie's mother could not provide a stable environment for her dependent children. Tyrannized by the demons within and over-whelmed by the stresses of mothercare, this woman was often out of control. Yet, in the midst of the chaos and violence that dominated her mother's household, little Annie found some solace and hope. An avid reader, she immersed herself in *The Little House on the Prairie* series and "adopted" its central characters, the Ingalls, as family. As Annie explained, "My mother was wild and unpredictable, but the Ingalls family was responsible and loving. Through my reading, I began to understand that my mother wasn't normal, that there was something very wrong with her. I also began to believe that when I was grown up, I could create a normal family—that there was no reason why I shouldn't build my own little house on the prairie."

I do not want to suggest that Annie was cured by virtue of her identification with a storybook family; Annie still fell into relationships that were chaotic and violent—but she did not seem permanently stuck in them. The ideal of the Ingalls family, which had become a part of her, at least suggested the possibility of a better life, which Annie was determined to make for herself.

Without a doubt, the most fortunate daughters among us were blessed during childhood with a nurturing, generous, life-loving mother. But those of us less fortunate can often compensate for early deprivations. The motherkiss comes in all forms and at all stages of life—the consistent care of a therapist, the kind acts of a teacher or other adult friend, even the printed pages of a children's story—and always it leaves a shining, indelible imprint on the spirit.

# CHAPTER 7

# *Mother Nature as Healer*

Gradually I came to sense the trees and lakes and wildflowers as a nurturant power. Wandering about in the rose garden one day I had an impression there was a presence in the garden. It seemed to be all around me, trying to get my attention.

—Kim Chernin
*Reinventing Eve: Modern Woman in Search of Herself*

In the previous chapter, I emphasized that sharing our deepest feelings with sympathetic others relieves anxieties and depressions. However, both my personal and clinical experiences have taught me that although loving human exchange can be wonderfully healing, it is not the only salve. For example, turning to Nature—the vital forces of plant and animal life—can also repair wounded hearts and souls. In order to heal, women who as children were un-mothered or under-mothered must learn ways to soothe themselves and to fill up the "holes" within that have resulted from early deprivations. A positive relationship with Nature is both soothing and filling.

Whenever I treat women who suffer the effects of poor early mothering, in addition to helping them make healthy human connections, I advise them to establish a relationship with Nature: to take solitary walks in Boulder's foothills or to follow the creek that meanders through the city; to plant and tend a small garden; to lie on the new grass; to sit under the stars on mild nights; to fill their rooms with living plants and flowers; to care for a pet. In my own case, when writing hour after hour, I unearth disturbing childhood memories that fill me with anxiety, I frequently leave my desk and wander in my backyard. I lie on the sweet-smelling grass, watch the movement of the clouds, follow the antics of a squirrel scurrying up the crabapple tree, or just close my eyes and allow the sun to wrap me in its warmth. Then, after a time, I am restored, filled up, ready to return to my writing.

By going into Nature, we experience a oneness with the universe, which relieves feelings of conflict and fragmentation. Outer experience changes inner experience: Harmony inherent in the natural world instills a lovely feeling of internal unity. Just as a soothing mother quells her young child's distress by containing her fears and anxieties, Mother Nature can be a source of solace for the adult child in pain.

Anne-Marie, whom I have counseled for several months, requested an emergency appointment. When she came to my office, she looked as if she had been through a war. An impending visit by her mother—a woman who had physically abused her during childhood—was stirring up massive anxiety, and Anne-Marie had spent the last few days alternating between crying fits and bouts of exhaustion. After our session, which was on a Friday, I suggested that she spend the weekend, which promised to be clear and mild, hiking in the Rockies and that on Monday we have another session. On Monday, however, Anne-Marie, who had always been prompt and reliable, did not show up. Most apologetic, she phoned me the next day to explain that she had "spaced out" our appointment. Her weekend retreat into the mountains had so rejuvenated her that the session planned for Monday proved unnecessary. Anne-Marie and I knew that she was not suddenly cured of her mother-wound, but we also knew that her time spent in the mountains had been somehow reparative—the pain within had subsided. Alone in the mountains, Anne-Marie had discovered a nurturant power.

Stephanie Demetrakopulos, writer and professor of women's studies, connects mountains to the spirit of very old women: deep-rooted, pondering, silent. She points out that certain women artists and writers seem to have a fascination with mountains. For example, in her poem "Phantasia For Elvira Shatayev," Adrienne Rich imagines the death of some women mountain climbers as a merging with the Mother. I am reminded as well of Georgia O'Keeffe's oils of the red, orange, and pink hills near Abiquiu, New Mexico, which evoke images of voluptuous, goddess forms emerging from the dusty earth.[1]

Whereas some women feel a special connection with the mountains, others are drawn to the sea and seashore for restoration. Perhaps the sea is a healing force because it stirs—at some deep, dark, unconscious level—the memory of having once been perfectly contained in the maternal waters of the womb. A journalist friend of mine, Lynn Malkinson, wrote that when she was pregnant and living near a beach in Mombassa, Kenya, far from home and her own parents, she once dug a hole in the wet sand to hold her stomach. Like a nurturing mother or grandmother, the sea sand cradled her and the baby within. Indeed, as researcher and writer Barbara G. Walker notes, the correspondence between the sea and Mother is universal; "Ma," the basic mother-syllable of Indo-European languages, is an ideogram for waves of water.[2]

Even grown-up, self-sufficient, and successful adults yearn from time to time to be relieved of adult pressures, to be simply children again. Anne Morrow Lindbergh describes the pull of the primeval rhythms of the sea to a more basic state of being.

Rollers on the beach, wind in the pines, the slow flapping of herons across sand dunes, drown out the hectic rhythms of city and suburb, time tables and schedules. One falls under their spell, relaxes, stretches out prone. One becomes, in fact, like the element on which one lies, flattened by the sea; bare, open, empty as the beach, erased by today's tides of all yesterday's scribblings.[3]

For some people, the natural world offers a respite from the demanding everyday world—a place to let down one's defenses. For others, the relationship with Nature is more sustaining. A colleague, who as a child had been consistently abused by all the adults in her family, once told me that her positive relationship to the earth was her salvation: "Had I grown up in a city rather than in the plains of New Mexico, I don't think I would have made it." Sitting in a doctor's office, I recently came upon a magazine article that describes Wyoming's Cheyenne Botanic Gardens project.[4] Here elderly people, teenagers on probation, mentally and physically impaired adults, and other interested community members roll up their sleeves and help make gardens grow. And as these volunteers transplant, water, prune, and fertilize, they themselves become changed. By nurturing the earth, they are in turn nurtured. Shane Smith, the director of the project comments, "We have a saying here that you take the bad out of the day with a shovel. . . . This looks like a greenhouse and smells like a greenhouse, but it's also a garden where people can grow."[5]

A number of scientific studies support the idea that tending plants and flowers heals our spirit. At Northampton VA Medical Center in Massachusetts, for example, patients who worked daily in the soil were able to reduce their medication and eliminate sleeping pills entirely.[6] Mental illness is a condition of inner deadness. In working the soil, which is rich in new growth, one reconnects to flourishing life.

Psychiatrist and author Anthony Storr suggests that people who never knew or who prematurely lost the good, protective, embracing mother of childhood may find a substitute through a fusion with Nature. He points to William Wordsworth, who, orphaned as a young child, describes Nature as

The anchor of my purest thoughts, the nurse
The guide, the guardian of my heart, and soul
Of all my moral being.[7]

Storr's suggestion helps me understand how my grandmother, who as a young girl watched her mother burn to death in a house fire, overcame her grief through a communion with Nature. When still in her teens, my grandmother—always an unconventional and free thinker—embraced pantheism, a philosophy that sees God and Nature as one. As a child I found it difficult to follow her explanations of this seemingly strange philosophy. What I do remember, however, is that Grandma invested all Nature with human characteristics. Moreover, she seemed to have a deeply personal relationship with plants and flowers, whose full Latin names she would recite to me as if they referred not to little growing things but rather to esteemed personages whom one might honor at an elegant dinner party. Indeed, when I close my eyes I can see her—a tiny round woman with white hair and spectacles—bending down to smile at and whisper greetings to the yellow snapdragons that managed to grow between the cracks of cement during New York City's short springtime.

I believe now that my grandmother became the cheerful, optimistic woman I loved so much partly because she had been able to form a spiritual relationship with the earth mother, the mother of vegetative life. In Mother Nature she seemed to find a partial substitute for the real mother lost too early. Of course, had my grandmother replaced all human relationships with her intense relationship to Nature, her life would have been limited. But she did not do this. Although she revered the harmony of the natural environment, she was also an active participant in the less tidy, more chaotic world of people. For her, Nature was a wonderful enabler rather than an escape from reality.

In my practice I have known several women who, suffering from physical or psychological mother loss, have formed a special relationship to Nature. Irene turned to Nature for mothering because her mother, who was a devoted musician, had little time or patience for Irene when she was growing up. Mother's house felt cold and unwelcoming; the outdoors became a haven for young Irene. During one of our sessions, Irene shared a poem that she had written at age twelve. In it the protective nurturing mother Irene never knew in reality emerges in the form of a tree—a symbol that connotes a rooted and sheltering maternal strength.

> I propped myself against the rough
> Gray bark of an old spruce tree,
> And closed my eyes, for the world that day
> Had not been kind to me.
> I closed my eyes with a little sigh,
> As the weary often will,
> And thought how good to lean on one
> So straight and strong and still!
> High up above, her branches moved
> Against the spacious sky,
> And little wandering breezes
> Played a gentle lullaby.
> Her branches showed a simple strength
> And silent sympathy.
> Tolerance . . . endurance . . . acceptance
> Flowed quietly from tree to me.

In many stories and folktales, characters turn to Nature to relieve the pain of mother loss. For example, the theme of Nature as substitute mother is woven through *The Wizard of Oz*. The gray, dry, and barren landscape of Kansas symbolizes Dorothy's withholding, psychologically absent mother, Aunt Em; the lush and abundant fields of Oz represent the good inner mother that she cultivates. Even the color of Emerald City—Dorothy's destination—suggests Nature's abundance: the green of bountiful crops.

Although women who have suffered the physical or psychological absence of mother may be especially drawn to the natural world, adult daughters blessed during childhood with a loving and present mother also benefit by increasing their ties to Nature. As we age, many of us find that we can turn less and less to our own mothers for care and concern. As our mother becomes older, she may increasingly need our attentions while becoming less available to us. Even when she does not depend on us for physical or emotional support, we may find her less involved in our lives. A sixty-five-year-old client remarked, "Having raised four children, I am too tired at this point to do any more parenting. I no longer want to get tangled in the life problems of my grown kids." When mother no longer mothers, we must find ways to mother ourselves, and Nature is an endless source of nurturance. Long before people ever "invented" psychotherapists, they turned to Mother Nature for solace.

I must confess that as I write about the healing possibilities of Nature, I am filled with some sadness. I cannot overlook the fact that for many—perhaps most—women, spending time alone at the seashore or walking in the woods or even sitting on a park bench is no longer safe. The violence rampant in our society has forced us to become vigilant and cautious. It seems that in order to enjoy the natural world, we must devise new strategies. I for one always make sure that I am with a companion—my husband or a woman friend—when I spend time in isolated places. We have learned to respect each other's private space, and even as we are walking side by side are able to go into ourselves and feel alone. I used to think that being in someone's company demanded a constant interchange. To be alone in the presence of another is a new freedom for me.

Other women have found more ingenious ways to enjoy Nature safely. One of my clients, who lived in a crime-ridden section of Denver and was particularly fearful about venturing away from home, decided to bring Nature indoors. Each evening she would retreat to her Nature Room—a tiny space filled with potted plants, vases brimming with fresh flowers, and an aquarium of tropical fish—to sit and muse. As she explained, "It would be lovely to feel free to take an evening stroll in the park. But I don't have that luxury, and so I have made do—quite nicely, I think."

Katharine Krueger, a colleague, points out that even when safety is not an issue, many women do not feel at home in Nature. Those who, for example, have lived only in cities must often learn to make a connection with the nonhuman environment. To this end, she sometimes recommends that her female clients buy a bouquet of flowers after sessions. As she explains,

> So many of my clients are uncomfortable in the natural world. If I suggested that they spend a weekend alone in the wilderness, they would likely feel threatened because they do not yet know how to relate in the outdoors. But buying flowers is a simple, nonthreatening thing for them to do, and inevitably they discover that flowers make them feel better. Plants, flowers, all vegetation are symbols of life and growth and the beauty that still abounds in our world.

Katharine Krueger's "flower therapy" reminds me of Georgia O'Keeffe's motivation for her flower paintings.

> A flower is relatively small. Everyone has many associations with a flower—the idea of flowers. You put out your hand to touch the flower—lean forward to smell it—maybe touch it with your lips—almost without thinking—or give it to someone to please them. Still—in a way—nobody sees a flower—really—it is so small—we haven't time—and to see takes time, like to have a friend takes time. If I could paint the flower exactly as I see it no one would see what I see because I would paint it small like the flower is small.
> So I said to myself—I'll paint what I see—what the flower is to me but I'll paint it big and they will be surprised into taking time to look at it—I will take time to make even busy New Yorkers take time to see what I see of flowers.[8]

Although being in Nature is a sensually rewarding experience, it can also stimulate the intellect. In my practice, I sometimes use examples from Nature to help clients gain new perspectives.

A few years ago I counseled Meg, who, as a result of having been sexually abused by her father and unprotected from these assaults by her mother, had developed an aggressive persona. Believing that people would never treat her fairly, Meg had developed an adversarial, confrontational style that alienated others. Meg's inability to make or to keep friends brought her into therapy.

At the time, I was reading Merlin Stone's interpretation of the *Tao Teh Ching*, which in great part is an observation and celebration of the wisdom of Nature. The *Tao Teh Ching* suggests that the activity of the water flowing around a great boulder provides a model of the feminine principle, the *yin*. Meg's feminine (gentle, yielding, receptive) side—her *yin*— was underdeveloped; she knew only how to respond aggressively. In fact, the students at the school in which she taught had unkindly nicknamed her "The Hammer" because, I suppose, an exchange with her felt much like a pounding.

In addition to talking about Meg's overly forceful, overly masculine personality style, I asked her to go after our session to Boulder Creek (one of the natural wonders of our beautiful city) and to pay special attention to the movement of the water: to notice that when the rushing water meets a boulder along its path, it does not continually crash against it but flows around this obstacle to make new paths. For Meg, the image of the brook and the boulder was powerful, one on which we often drew during the course of therapy. More than the wordy explanations I had provided, this image helped Meg see that ramming against people undermined her and that it is sometimes more effective to go around them, much the way the running water goes around the large rocks that stand in its way.

Becoming less confrontational, Meg discovered that people were more open to her and that friendly relationships were indeed possible. Moreover, she understood that she did not have to pound her ideas into their heads in order to be respected but could present them in a gentler, more feminine way.

I am quite convinced that by turning to Nature as teacher—just as the ancient Chinese and the American Indians did—women can deepen the meaning of their lives and also discover universal, time-honored solutions for the problems that beset them. The Navajo referred to the processes of Nature as Changing Woman, and, as Merlin Stone describes:

It is Changing Woman who teaches the flow of life, the restlessness of the sand as it flies in the wind, the wisdom of the ancient rocks that never leave their home, the pleasure of the sapling that had risen through them. . . .

It is Changing Woman who teaches the cycles, the constant round of hot and cold, of birth and dying, of youth and aging, of seedling to corn, of corn to seedling kernel, of day to night, of night to day, of waxing moon to waning moon. . . .

It is to Changing Woman that we look as we search for the wisdom of life.[9]

Nature is indeed a changing woman. Sometimes she is gentle and soothing, but at other times she is hard, fierce, and demanding. Her two-sidedness is characteristic of the growth-enhancing mother who is compassionate and nurturing but, when necessary, also firm, tough-minded, and demanding.[10] Just as the enhancing flesh and blood mother does not overprotect her child but pushes her to meet life's challenges, Mother Nature provides her children with myriad opportunities to become strong and capable: She offers trees and rocks and mountains to climb, fields to run across, lakes to swim in, ocean waves to jump. By passing nature's tests of our physical strength, we are empowered.

*          *          *

Growing up in New York City, I never learned how to ride a bike or climb a tree. Moreover, because my grandmother thought that the other children who lived in our neighborhood were "ruffians," she did not allow me to jump rope or play other street games with them. No wonder that I grew up to be very unathletic. When I was seventeen, my best girlfriend, Geri, and I decided to visit Colorado on our own. Much less timid than I and always ready for a new adventure, Geri signed us up for a three-day mountain climbing expedition. At her urging, we hid the fact from our guide that we were wholly inexperienced. And when, at the end of the first day's climb, he advised those climbers who were having difficulty breathing to set up camp instead of push ahead, we managed to cover up the fact that we were gasping for air. "Just hold your breath whenever he gets too close," Geri whispered, and I agreed that this was a wonderful plan. Increasingly determined not to let a mountain get the better of us, we two city girls pressed on and did indeed manage to reach its peak.

To be sure, for days after the climb, I was ill from exhaustion, and because I had not used sunscreen, looked like a monster from the deep with my swollen lips and a burned, peeling face. But despite this and the fact that I had been foolishly reckless to climb a mountain without the requisite skills, I felt wonderfully proud of myself. After more than twenty-five years, that feeling of triumph—having climbed *my* Little Mount Matterhorn—has not entirely worn off. I can easily understand why programs such as Outward Bound, which encourage young people to master the challenges of the natural environment, succeed in raising their self-esteem and self-confidence. The affirmations—recognition of one's good power and competence—that cannot be found through human relationships can sometimes be found in relationship to Nature.

*          *          *

Until now, I have dwelt on the inanimate aspects of Nature. But just as the sea and the earth can revivify women, animals can benefit them also. As Marie-Louise von Franz, a student of C. J. Jung and a noted scholar in her own right, explains:

Women have a very deep relationship to nature in its positive form. Relationships to animals can also effect the cure and many women make a relationship to a pet, which at that time may mean more to them than anything else because its unconscious simplicity appeals to the wounds within them. Relationship to a human is a differentiated task; but relationship to an animal is simple, and in feeling for it, the lost tenderness may be discovered.[11]

The sweet love Dorothy of *The Wizard of Oz* shows for her little dog, Toto, illustrates how a relationship with a pet can compensate for less than adequate relationships with human beings.

It was Toto that made Dorothy laugh, and saved her from growing as gray as her other surroundings. Toto was not gray; he was a little black dog, with long, silky hair and small black eyes that twinkled merrily on either side of his funny, wee nose. Toto played all day long, and Dorothy played with him, and loved him dearly.[12]

Sometimes the mere *idea* of a relationship with a little animal can be healing. When I was a little girl, I was not allowed a dog or a cat because the New York City apartment in which I lived with my parents and grandparents was already overcrowded. On my daily walks in the park with my grandmother, I dragged along a limb from a tree that became my imaginary puppy. Because I was an only child without friends my own age, it was with my stick-dog— which I envisioned as soft, furry, and fully accepting of me— that I often carried on animated conversations and shared secrets.

I always hoped that my own children would be luckier than I had been and have a real dog or cat as companion, but their allergies to animal dander thwarted such a plan. During a visit to his grandmother's home in Florida, however, my son was presented with a little turtle, which he grew to love deeply. Like a devoted—perhaps overprotective—mother, Jon could not bear the idea of leaving his turtle behind when we vacationed, and so Dribble, housed in a Tupperware container of water, stones, and shredded lettuce, accompanied us on a plane trip to New York City and an auto ride to Cape Cod. This little creature, which hardly did more than peek his head out of his shell from time to time, elicited Jon's most tender feelings and, I suspect, developed in him a reverence for all living things.

Whereas most of us recognize the need children have to care for a pet, we commonly ignore the benefits that an attachment to an animal can provide adults. More than providing companionship, caring for an animal can soften the heart. A colleague, Dr. Carol E. Ryan, points out, human relationships can be unpredictable and, at times, cruel, but loving a pet is safe: "The world of people may rebuff or act indifferently, but a dog rewards her caretaker with unconditional loyalty."

In addition to giving love, pets are able also to accept it from us, which in turn makes us feel worthy. I recall the words of one client, a woman victimized by parental, then spousal, abuse.

The people who were primary to me didn't have much respect for life. Much of the time I feel pretty worthless myself. What gives my life value are my animals. I know I would spend my last cent on them. Loving my birds, my fish, my two dogs as I do, I sometimes am filled with a feeling that all life is precious—even mine.

I think too that certain pets bring out a latent playfulness in women. Typically, from the time they are quite small, females have been taught not to romp, not to be boisterous, not to be too physical. Horseplay and rowdy behavior are allowed fathers and sons, not mothers and daughters. In the past, proper mothers taught their little girls to squelch their lively natures in favor of more refined ones. But it is hardly possible for a woman to be staid in the company of a frisky puppy, for example. In *An Unknown Woman*, an autobiographical novel about a woman who, in order to overcome a childhood of inadequate mothering and a lifetime of depression, retreats to Nantucket during the dead of winter, Alice Koller describes how a puppy, her sole companion, brings her to life.

Logos, prepared for his morning race across the yard, stops paw-deep in snow on the stone stoop, then retreats into the kitchen next to me. I kneel to reassure him. "Logos, that's snow!" I hold the door open for him to try again. He dips one paw into the cold whiteness, immediately lifts it out again, and holds it in the air for me to do something about.

"Okay, I'll show you what snow is for." I fly upstairs, pursued by the puzzled puppy, and put on my clothes so fast that legs and pants, arms and sleeves, boots and feet seem utterly mismatched for one another. Buttons and buttonholes on my coat fare no better. The unfamiliar speed keeps Logos intent on my every gesture, so that, when I reach down to make the first snowball of the year, his nose follows my hand into the snow. I shape the ball, talking. . . . A cry gurgles in his throat. Every inch of him is ready.

"Shall I throw it?"

Two high-pitched yelps reply. I sling the ball the width of the yard, and Logos runs so fast that he catches it at the exact spot where it lands. He eats the thing that dissolves before his jaws move twice. He turns to me astonished. I laugh out loud to watch him move his lips and tongue, and know how cool his interior has become, how incredulous he is of his whole experience. All at once he takes up a mouthful of snow and eats it with abandon. He thrusts his nose down and keeps it in the snow. He's on to something lying deep in that very spot. Or is it there, there, or there? His nose vacuums the entire front lawn, and the rear of him follows ridiculously along, his tail sweeping widely back and forth in joy. . . . In the kitchen making coffee, I watch him from the window. What was the last thing I did that filled me with that kind of delight? I think and think, but somehow I'm unable to remember.[13]

One of the most destructive effects of poor mothering can be a child's feelings of disconnection from her self. When the unempathic mother fails to recognize and resonate with the growing child's real feelings, the child herself begins to feel unreal and to mistrust her perceptions. She is not in touch with her inner life—her intuitive sense or instincts—but is rather cut off from it. Instead of trusting her intuitions, the wounded daughter turns to outside sources to tell her how she should feel. This was the case for Alice Koller, who had existed for thirty-seven years never knowing what *she* wanted, who experienced herself only as a reflection in other people's eyes.

If a woman is to be whole, she must make a connection to her own instinctual life. Psychological health depends on her ability to trust herself. And sometimes animals—which are all instinct, all spontaneity—can help a woman do this. In a relationship with animals, a woman may begin to feel and to accept her own animal nature: what is basic and visceral. Alice Koller teaches Logos "what snow is for," and, in the process, this little dog teaches Alice to feel her own feelings, to discover her self, to know the deep pleasure of being fully alive.

It is not only small animals that promote well-being. In Boulder County and its surrounding area we have many ranches, and several of my female clients are accomplished riders. Within the last few years, I have become increasingly aware that a woman's relationship with a horse has great potential for healing maternal woundings.

Lori, the daughter of a remarkably unempathic mother
and a passive father, was in her thirties when she gave up
her financially successful business as an entrepreneur,
moved to a farm with her husband, and bought a horse.
Subject to severe depressions, she found that riding was
wonderfully restorative, perhaps even more potent than the
antidepressants that had been prescribed for her: "After I
have been out riding in the fields, I feel great. The world is
right with me, and I understand bliss."

During one session Lori presented the following dream,
which vividly points to the deep healing possible between
a woman and her horse.

> I saw a horse spitting out my sister. Although my sister
> had an adult head, her shape was that of an embryo still
> in its sac. I knew that my sister was "ungestated" and
> needed more time. My husband appeared and together we
> lifted my sister back on to the horse.

In our interpretation, Lori and I came to believe that the
sister, who in reality had been physically abused by Lori's
mother, was a stand-in for Lori. Although Lori had not been
corporally punished as a child, she had been wounded by
her mother's tactless, often cruel, remarks. Moreover, having
witnessed her sister's beatings, one might say that Lori was
indirectly abused. Every child necessarily identifies with her
siblings and to some degree feels their pain. A parent's injustices toward one child are experienced by all the children
in the family.

The image of the embryo still in its sac suggested that Lori
was yet unformed, incomplete. Indeed, in our sessions she
often revealed a crisis of identity: "I don't know who I am,
Dr. Bassoff. I feel somehow unfinished, as if I've never become who I am meant to be." As is so often the case, poorly
mothered daughters have an impaired sense of self. As we
have seen, a child needs to have her inner experiences rec-
ognized in order to feel real. From Lori's reports of her
childhood, it was clear that her mother, who appears to have

been adequately maternal during her daughter's infancy, was not able to show tender feelings toward Lori as she got older. Just as in the dream the horse spat out the embryo, so in life Lori's mother had pushed her out of the warm, embracing mother's realm too early. Although the symbolism of the horse is extremely complex and various, Jung suggests that it represents, among other things, "the mother within us," that is, intuitive understanding.[14] Certainly Lori's dream imagery reflected a very strong correspondence between horse and mother.

To me, Lori's dream seemed very hopeful because it indicated that with the blessing of time, with the support of her good husband, she would reach completion. Her instruction was simple: "Get back on the horse."

Lori's story and those of other clients lead me to believe that the relationship between a woman and her horse can help compensate for early failures of maternal empathy. In order for the horse and rider to move smoothly, each must be exquisitely aware of the other, sensitive to the other's vibrations, tensions, emotions, and moods. The harmonious movement of an accomplished rider and her horse mimics the "fit" that is ideally found in the earliest mother-child relationship; Marshall H. Klaus and John H. Kennel, who do research with infants, have described this linking as a synchronized dance between mother and infant.[15] I think it is reasonable to assume that women who as infants or young children were "out of step" with their mothers may create through a relationship with a horse new and marvelous feelings of union and harmony.

In addition to the experience of inner balance, accomplished horsemanship often provides women with an experience of their own strength and mastery. As I elaborated in earlier chapters, women are disabled not only by unempathic mothers but by powerless ones—women who have failed to achieve and to take control of their own lives. Without strong mothers as role models, daughters are likely to inhibit their own desires for personal power. And, as accumulating research demonstrates, depression derives in great part from feelings of helplessness, ineffectualness, and incompetence. But surely the girl or woman who takes hold of the reins and learns to control the mighty horse will taste—perhaps for the first time—her own wonderful power. Sitting high and erect, how can she not feel masterful and proud? Moreover, her power will have a special *yin* quality. As every good rider knows, a horse will not respond well to force, aggression, or brutality but rather to a strength that is paradoxically gentle: specifically, a woman's strength.

As I conclude this chapter about the natural world—its plant and animal life, its landscapes of forest, desert, plain, hills, mountain, and sea—as a source of healing, I cannot help but observe that we humans have exploited it; I cannot help worry that we are destroying our good earth. On my daily walks in Fort Tryon Park with my grandmother, we used to pass an area of carefully tended flower gardens—a small paradise in the hustle and bustle of New York City. Although it is thirty years since I last visited the gardens, I remember the words on the wooden sign at their entrance: "Let no one say and say it to your shame that all was beauty until you came."[16] It is easy to despair, to feel helpless as we read about acts of vandalism, toxic waste, the greenhouse effect, acid rain, the extinction of plants and animals. It is harder, but absolutely necessary, to change our habits of waste and pillage: to treat, in our own small ways, our ailing Mother Earth, who nurtures us and makes us whole, with the care and gentleness she so deserves.

# CHAPTER 8

# Creative Transformations: The Pen and the Paintbrush

Creativity is the encounter of the intensively conscious human being with his or her world.
—Rollo May
*The Courage to Create*

A characteristic of our humanness is the need to make sense of the world rather than perceive it as chaotic, random, and out of control. Looking at amorphous shapes of clouds, for example, we see faces, animals, or snowy landscapes; watching the star-filled sky, we decipher the outlines of mythological beasts and gods. Similarly, by organizing and finding meaning in our personal life—even our worst sufferings—we gain mastery over it. In this chapter, I will show how through creative activities—drawing, painting, writing, composing—we can enlarge the meanings of our life and transform inner turmoil into something coherent.

Unfortunately, many people believe that creativity, rather than being a basic endowment, is the sole property of geniuses or eccentrics. It is true that only the most gifted among us produce great works of art, but this fact should not discourage the rest of us from realizing our creative potential.[1] Yet, all too often, when I suggest that a client write a poem or paint a picture of her confusion or sadness or anger or joy, she responds, "Oh, I couldn't do that. I'm not a creative person." Believing that the art they would like to make will not be good enough to hang above the mantelpiece or that the stories they dream of writing will have little chance of being published, women often inhibit their creative efforts; hence, they never reap the reward of achieving the sense of purpose and meaningfulness that is inherent in the creative process.

When I was a college student majoring in art, I came to realize—quite accurately—that I did not have the talent to become a first-rate artist, and so I changed my major to education and for a time refused to draw or paint. Without my art work, however, I felt at loose ends. From early childhood on, drawing had meant more than producing something to hang on a wall. Instead, it was my way of apprehending the world, of engaging it, of transforming it. My real childhood world—shaped by my parents' experience of the Holocaust—was not always comprehensible to me, and in it I often felt small, confused, and afraid. But whenever I drew a flower, a house, a feeling, or my mother's face, I began to make sense out of this confusion and to know my environment. By making pictures out of the jumble of people, things, ideas, feelings, and sensations that impinged on me, I was no longer the helpless child *being done to;* rather, during these moments of creativity, I was *shaper* and *communicator* of my reality. The world that often felt alien and dangerous to me became more approachable, and in it I felt less afraid. For me drawing was much more than a pleasurable pastime: It was therapy.

If, as a college student, I had been less self-demanding, less intent on meeting self-imposed standards of excellence, I would not have given up the artistic efforts that had helped me make a better relationship to the world. Similarly, if certain of my clients were less perfectionistic and less worried about being judged, they might try their hand at painting or writing or composing and thereby realize the joys of creative work. My own daughter—who has escaped the tyranny of perfectionism—came home from a dance class recently all aglow. "You must be doing very well," I commented. "No," she laughed, "I'm the *klutziest* person in my dance class, but I'm loving it anyway!"

Some women inhibit creative expression because they are afraid of being judged unfavorably; others do so because they are wary of confronting and exposing their inner life, especially if it holds dark secrets. After my friend Jenny decided to write a book about the impact incest had on her life, she was immobilized by anxiety. As she shared, "I was hurt so badly as a child. Now I am afraid that by making new contact with my weeping, broken child, I will be hurt all over again." My friend's fears are justifiable. As we break down our defenses—the rationalizations, denials, and fantasies that protect us against knowing all the truth of our past—we are left raw and vulnerable. Pain first gets worse, not better, with awareness—and the creative act insists that we become self-aware.[2] Yet, if we persist in telling our life story (through our art work, writings, music, dance, or drama), if we push through the initial pain of self-discovery, we will gradually hurt less.

When I began writing *Mothering Ourselves*, I too was anxious and unsure. I dreaded having to encounter the scared, anxiety-ridden, hypochondrical little girl I once was, for she embarrassed me and made me cry. Moreover, I worried that in telling about my childhood, I would hurt my mother. Was I justified in exposing parts of her life in order to write about my own? Nevertheless, trusting that the potential good outweighed the bad, I am writing my story. And yes, I am glad for it.

Creative activity heals in a variety of ways. The following vignette illustrates how it helped Paula, a married woman in her early forties with three small children, develop a fuller sense of selfhood. Although Paula's story is unique, I hope that it will inspire my readers to take their own creative leaps.

From early childhood Paula had been rejected by her

mother, a woman with seemingly little capacity for human relationship, and largely ignored by her father, an exceedingly passive man. When Paula first came to see me, she was suicidally depressed, although at a loss to articulate the source of her despair. Despite her low energy and without formal training in art, Paula was nevertheless open to the suggestion that she "paint" her inner experiences. As I noted in an earlier chapter, in an effective therapy a "mute" client is transformed into a talking one: In order to heal our wounds, we must first *name* them. Although Paula could not find words to communicate her pain, she was able to give it form through her paintings, which she did not hesitate to share with me.

Her first painting depicted a tiny swimmer drowning in a bowl of viscous pea soup. Although this painting reflected Paula's feelings of being overwhelmed by family obligations, it was her first small step toward becoming whole. As a child, Paula had learned to hide her feelings, partly because emotional reactions—especially signs of need or frailty, but also expressions of childish spontaneity—offended her mother. Like Dorothy's Aunt Em in *The Wizard of Oz*, Paula's "gray" mother seemed to recoil at her child's vivid responses to life. "Now don't get excited," she would usually say when Paula showed emotion, "just learn to control yourself." Understandably, the adult Paula wore a stiff upper lip; frequently, she told me, "I don't understand why I am suicidal. I have nothing to complain about." But if Paula was emotionally inhibited, her "soup painting" was most expressive. "Look," it screamed out, "I am not the in-control, take-charge woman I've pretended to be. I am a tiny swimmer about to drown in a sea of family obligations. Help me!" Through her art work, Paula began to express the vulnerable parts of herself that she had kept hidden too long.

Paula's second painting was of a house. Whereas some of the rooms were cheery and well-lit, others were dark or locked up. Both of us understood that the black, barred rooms represented the hidden, "unacceptable" emotional parts of Paula—the panic and fear, insecurity, shame, and rage as well as the playfulness and joie de vivre. Other paintings followed: of lonely trees battered by the wind; studies of the color gray; and then, as Paula's depression eased, landscapes of gently rolling hills under spots of blue sky. At Christmas time, Paula presented me with a photocopy of one of her paintings entitled "Courage"—a dark background with a single white line skipping, dancing, soaring.

In the early chapters of this book, I dwelt on wounds a mother inflicts on her child when the mother cannot look upon *all* of her with basic approval. Paula's mother—so shut off from her own feelings—failed to empathize with her daughter's normal fears and worries as well as with her exuberance. In order not to risk disapproval, Paula had learned to close off these human sides of herself and to assume an unemotional persona. Through her paintings, however, Paula expressed all parts of her self, which allowed her to feel increasingly vital and whole. By bringing to life those aspects previously deadened, she gradually lifted herself out of depression.

During a therapy session, Paula expressed the pleasure that ran through her whenever she looked at the living room wall covered with her paintings. One time she told me that when she beheld all her work, she could not help but giggle to herself. I suggested that it must be an awesome feeling knowing that each of these paintings represented another aspect of her rich and unique life, to which Paula exclaimed, "Yes, that's the meaning of the giggle!"

Paula was never much interested in public showings of her work. Indeed, she told me that she could not bear the thought of selling one of her paintings.

It has taken me so long to create a whole, full, vital self. Every painting portrays an aspect of *me*: my fears, my despair, my serenity, my joy. Selling a painting to a stranger would feel like giving up a piece of myself; I would feel as if part of me were cut off.

I suspect, however, that sharing her art work with me was healing. I did what her mother had been unable to do: By virtue of approval of and interest in Paula's paintings, I mirrored her unique, multifaceted self-experience. Through her artistic creativity—giving form to her emotional experiences—and my affirmations, Paula could begin to heal.

Adult daughters who as children are blessed with an affirming—a *kvelling*—mother are fortunate; for them, feelings of self-acceptance usually come quite easily. But I have discovered that inner troubles rather than happiness, feelings of deprivation rather than of completeness, can be the powerful springs of inventiveness and imagination. Of course, I would not suggest that childhood adversity is desirable; yet a certain amount of discontent seems to jog our creative impulses. It was Jung who wisely said, "Man needs difficulties; they are necessary for health."[3] To be sure, too many difficulties can overwhelm and lead to defensive symptoms or a paralysis of the will, but an optimal amount of distress can help move us forward.

Just as Paula enlarged the meaning of her personality and life experiences by painting her previously hidden sides, Dorothy of *The Wizard of Oz* undergoes a transformation as she encounters and integrates the underdeveloped, "dangerous," and "unacceptable" parts of her self. Along the yellow brick road, she befriends a brainless Scarecrow, heartless Tin Woodman, and cowardly Lion, who represent the intelligence, compassion, and courage she must develop in herself. She also encounters an array of menacing monsters and beasts, among them, the growling Kalidahs with bodies like bears and heads like tigers; a pack of great wolves with fierce and sharp teeth; and, most unforgettable, the cadre of fearsome Winged Monkeys. These monsters symbolize the primitive forces of Dorothy's unconscious—her raw instincts and emotions. Dorothy transforms her self as she confronts these forces and brings them under her own power.

Through the creative process we encounter all aspects of the soul. In our paintings or written works, we safely express what we are forbidden to act out in real life, and, as we do this, we become more alive. May Sarton emphasizes this idea when she explains that through her poetry she is able "to break through to below the level of reason where the angels and monsters that the amenities keep in the cellar" come out to dance, to rove, to roar, to growl, and to sing.[4] Traditionally, women are discouraged from expressing anything that is not "nice" or socially acceptable. Those emotional "monsters" imprisoned in the cellar do not, however, behave themselves but instead cause all manner of problems. For example, they take the form of splitting headaches, stomach and back pains, and "bitchy" moods. In contrast, the monsters released through our music, dances, writings, and paintings are benign. In fact, in Sarton's words, they "bring life back to the enclosed rooms where too often we are only . . . partly living."[5]

The creative process is healing only if we create (as Paula did) what is true for us, what reflects, deepens, and enriches the meaning of our lives. We must make a relationship with our own monsters and angels; in the moment that we alter our creations in order to please another or in order to conform to standards of acceptability, we develop "the false self"—the self that complies with others' wishes at the expense of losing its vitality.[6] Recently, a sad, overly compliant little girl confided, "My mom always sews my costumes for Halloween. This year, I really, really wanted to go as a rock star, maybe Madonna, but she thinks I should be a beautiful fairy princess, so that's what I'll be."

In a similar vein, one of my clients, who is a gifted artist, admitted that she feels uncomfortable creating pieces that reflect her inner experience. Instead she makes objects that others will find useful.

Friends seem to appreciate my woven place mats and decorative pillows, which I give as Christmas presents. But I am afraid that if I gave—or even showed—them my sketches, they would secretly sneer at me. I know that I have more or less stopped creating *real* art because I am afraid of rejection.

In addition to anxieties around rejection, the commitment to create can stir up other kinds of self doubts. Paula, more than once, questioned the rightness of her creative efforts: "I worry sometimes that painting is an indulgence. Instead of spending hours painting, I think maybe I should be folding the laundry or whipping up a batch of cookies—doing something *useful*." When another client of mine, a single working woman in her early forties with a talent for writing witty letters (a good number, in fact, about her outrageously self-centered mother), bought a typewriter for herself, she described it as a "subversive act." As Jill explained, "The typewriter will enable me to do all sorts of writing for my pleasure. But I feel rather *illegal* allowing myself such pleasure." Indeed, for a few weeks after the typewriter had been delivered to her home, Jill dared not use it. The symbol of the forbidden pleasure of creativity, it sat on its glossy new table untouched.

Women have a terrible time giving themselves permission to create and claiming for themselves what Henry James calls, "this dear old blessed healing."[7] Recently I discovered in Tillie Olsen's *Silences* the following passage by a little-known writer named Elizabeth Stuart Lyon Phelps. Written more than a century ago, Phelps's observations nevertheless reflect the condition of contemporary women.

> "When the fall sewing is done," "When the baby can walk," "When the housecleaning is over," "When the company has gone," "When we have got through with the whooping-cough," "When I am a little stronger," then I will write the poem, or learn the language, or study the great charity, or master the symphony; then I will act, dare dream, become.[8]

When a woman lives only in relationship, she becomes alienated from her inner resources. If a woman is to lay claim to her creative life, she must from time to time push away the demands of others and allow herself solitude, which is a necessary condition for creativity. Yet although women have a great capacity for being in relationship, they often have an undeveloped one for being in solitude. Women and men alike have been socialized to think that it is somehow unnatural or pitiful for a woman to be alone and selfish of her to enjoy her aloneness.

Years ago, when I was teaching in an elementary school, my colleagues and I took our lunch together. One teacher on the floor, however, rarely joined us. When I asked her why, she answered that the lunch hour was her "alone time," a time to sit and muse. My immediate reaction to this woman was disapproving. If she had told me that she spent lunch hours tutoring a pupil with special needs or meeting her husband at the local diner or visiting her mother in the hospital or even grading papers, I would have completely understood. But to refuse her colleagues' company in order to *sit and muse* seemed unfriendly, to say the least!

It is only in recent years that I have come to nurture my own solitude. I am learning that in order to create, I must alternate between an active engagement with the world and a retreat from it. The French essayist Michel de Montaigne addressed the need for temporary seclusion when he wrote, "We must reserve a little back shop, all our own, entirely free, wherein to establish our true liberty and principal retreat and solitude."[9] Coming to understand the importance of solitude in my own life, I encourage my clients to create their "little back shop" of quiet repose in which self-discovery can establish itself. In order to accomplish this, however, they must learn not only to feel entitled to their solitude but also to overcome the fear of being alone. In a culture that sees interpersonal relationship as the only source of happiness, many of us are afraid of being alone. Writer Anne Morrow Lindbergh elaborates this idea.

> How one hates to think of oneself as alone. How one avoids it. It seems to imply rejection or unpopularity. . . . We seem so frightened today of being alone that we never let it happen. Even if family, friends, and movies should fail, there is still the radio or television to fill up the void. . . .

Now instead of planting our solitude with dream blossoms, we choke the space with continuous music, chatter, and companionship to which we do not even listen. . . . When the noise stops there is no inner music to take its place. We must re-learn to be alone.[10]

I am in agreement with Lindbergh that we must relearn to be alone. For a good number of women, however, the prospect of being alone triggers a great panic fear, much like the terror of the small child who is separated from mother. Yet it is my experience that if a woman "practices solitude"— for short periods at first, then gradually longer ones—she will overcome this separation anxiety. "I feel so proud of myself," a recently divorced client said. "I went to a lovely restaurant *alone*. No conversation with a dinner partner, just my own thoughts and feelings to keep me company."

The initial terror and gradual calm acceptance of the solitary condition are vividly portrayed in *The Wizard of Oz*. Because creative expression springs from one's solitude, it is fitting that Dorothy's creative transformation begins when she is swept up by a cyclone and transported, all alone (save for her little dog), to the Land of Oz.

The house whirled around two or three times and rose slowly through the air. . . .

Hour after hour passed away, and slowly Dorothy got over her fright; but she felt quite lonely, and the wind shrieked so loudly all about her that she nearly became deaf. At first she had wondered if she would be dashed to pieces when the house fell again; but as the hours passed and nothing terrible happened, she stopped worrying and resolved to wait calmly and see what the future would bring.[11]

It seems that the only way to desensitize oneself to the fear of aloneness is to encounter it and, like Dorothy, discover that nothing terrible will happen—and, I should like to add, that something wonderful might happen: In solitude we may give birth to our creative potential and allow our "dream blossoms" to unfold.

As Paula's experience illustrates, the creative process is healing when it encourages us to recognize all parts of ourselves—even those parts we had disowned. By paying attention to our life experience—giving it form—we necessarily affirm its significance; we imbue our life with new meaningfulness and dignity. But the creative process is healing in yet another way. When we create, we transcend our own experience; we are actually able to transform past and present hurts into joy.

Paula once told me that while it was sadness that stirred her to paint her subjects, in the act of painting, she was rarely sad. "I concentrate so hard on getting the colors or the perspective just right, that I can't feel depressed when I'm painting. Instead of feeling depleted, I'm excited and involved in my work." The soothing mother of childhood regulates our emotions when they threaten to overwhelm us; she lulls, reassures, pacifies, cheers, and even distracts us from painful stimuli. Similarly, creative work absorbs our attentions so that we no longer wallow in our sorrow. The energy that was absorbed by our sorrow is now transformed into a different kind of energy—what Sarton describes as "a certain kind of imaginative energy [that lifts] the sufferer right out of himself into the joys of creation."[12]

The "magic" of the creative process is this power of transformation. As the artist creates a story, a poem, a picture, a dance, or a song, she also recreates herself; she is no longer the passive, helpless target of injustices but the engaged, active creator of her reality. My husband, Bruce—who often laughs joyously while he composes at the computer—describes how writing changes him.

> I often begin to write out of rage. My indignation and anger about life's injustices actually fuel my ideas for characters and plots. But in the process of writing, those feelings no

longer trammel me but propel me—like nets that have
tightened themselves into a trampoline: I am energized, I
am empowered. As my work comes alive, I too feel vibrant
and vivid. My anger has turned into something joyful,
funny, and even beautiful.

Paradoxically, at the same time that the creative experience
frees us, it also contains us, much like the protective, embracing mother of childhood. In America today, we tend
to scoff at restraints, espousing instead a philosophy of endless possibility. At a conference, Irvin Yalom, who teaches
at Stanford, once joked that in southern California, fast-food
stands sell hot dogs that come with the traditional plastic
packet of mustard, but instead of directions to "Tear open
at the dotted line," these read, "Tear anywhere!" When we
create, however, we cannot tear anywhere but are forced
into an organizing structure—whether the plot of a story,
the meter and rhyme of a poem, the time of a musical piece,
or the frame of a canvas. The "rules" of our craft allow us
to feel safe; we are contained even as we confront powerful
feelings; we are held even as we explore.

As I noted at the beginning of this chapter, many people
are intimidated by creative activity. Although during childhood most of us made up tunes and lyrics, painted pictures,
invented dances, wrote stories and poems, as time went on
we may have cut ourselves off from such marvelous expressions. But it is possible for us as adults to relearn how to be
creative. Above my desk I have a passage from the German
poet and playwright Johann Wolfgang von Goethe. When I
am feeling insecure as a writer, I turn to it and am encouraged. Goethe writes that there is a basic truth, the neglect
of which kills countless splendid ideas and plans: The moment we commit to create, we are blessed with divine guidance; all sorts of things occur that we never dreamed
possible. Whatever we can do or fancy we can do, we are
wise to begin—to begin now—for our boldness is the source
of genius, power, and magic.[13]

When I counsel women who are hesitant to initiate a project because they are unsure of themselves, I recall Goethe's instruction: Begin it now. In *The Courage to Create*, Rollo May writes: "We cannot will to have insights. We cannot *will* creativity. But we can *will* to give ourselves to the encounter with intensity of dedication and commitment."[14] The moment we commit ourselves—to begin it—we are embarked. In the hope that it will be helpful to other women, allow me to describe my beginnings as a writer.

I began to write my first book mainly because I needed to make sense out of my feelings of loss and anxiety as my teenage daughter liberated herself from our close-knit family. To be sure, when I started this project, I had little idea how to write a book. I had written journal articles, which were informative and objective, but had not, since my class in freshman composition, written a personal piece. Nevertheless, one Friday evening at the dinner table I surprised myself and made a grand pronouncement to my husband and children: "I have decided to write a book!" They looked up, nodded approvingly, resumed eating their spaghetti with red sauce, and moved the conversation to more immediate issues, such as how the New York Yankees were faring.

The next morning I woke up with contradictory feelings of excitement and dread: "How wonderful, today I start my book!" and "What am I getting myself into?" After reading Goethe's quote for inspiration, I cleared off my desk, set a fresh legal pad on it, and picked up a pen. Despite several hours of sitting and concentrating, I managed to squeeze out only a few lines. Certainly, I did not have much to show for the time spent writing, but nevertheless I felt vital— feelings that the experience of being fully engaged always brings. What was new and quite wonderful for me was the awareness that I was doing something just for myself; my writing project belonged to me alone. Not surprisingly, this awareness also generated some guilt: the feeling that creative work is selfish. But, with my husband's (and children's) encouragement, I began to set aside blocks of uninterrupted time to research my topic and to write. When I wrote, I still did not know exactly what I was doing or exactly where I was going, but, to my surprise, something began taking shape. And, as it did, I became even more involved with my project. Eager to get to the computer (which had eventually replaced legal pads and pens) with a fresh idea or a lovely phrase, I felt much like an infatuated young woman as she encounters her lover. What was first a mere impulse to write now had become a devotion, a passion. In fact, creating sometimes felt like a powerful religious experience. During my most productive times, I felt a force within—a wise and beautiful presence that was me and at the same time was not me—and she became my guide and blessed me with insights.

However, looking back, I cannot say that writing has been a consistently pleasurable experience. I have suffered the paralysis of writer's block (the abandonment by my beneficent muse); I have gone through periods of painful self-doubt, of frustration, and of exhaustion. Moreover, writing—my muse was benevolent but also a demanding taskmistress—absorbed so much of my time that I often had too little left for leisure. Still, I am glad for my efforts. When little Dorothy is about to embark on the yellow brick road, the good Witch warns her that it is a long journey "through a country that is sometimes pleasant and sometimes terrible."[15] But had Dorothy never taken the yellow brick road, the Scarecrow might never have gotten his wonderful brains and might have passed his whole life in a farmer's cornfield; the Tin Woodman might never have gotten his lovely heart but would have rusted in the forest; the Lion might have remained a coward forever; and Dorothy herself would not have grown.

Similarly, had I never made the grand pronouncement, "I have decided to write a book!" I might never have achieved a better understanding of my shifting, at times painful, relationships to my adolescent daughter, my aging mother, my grandmother, and myself. I am changed now. I feel older and wiser. But I feel younger too, connected once more to the child I was: the little girl who studied and came to know the world that confused her by drawing pictures of it.

\*     \*     \*

I am aware that undertaking a major artistic project requires the luxury of uninterrupted time and financial support—resources unavailable to many women. Certainly, I
could not have written my book while I was raising small
children, who necessarily required enormous amounts of
attention, or while I was teaching elementary school in
Harlem or doing graduate work or embarking on a career
as a psychotherapist—occupations that demanded most of
my energy. Recognizing that ample time and money are
necessary for major creative undertakings, I would be
reckless to advise clients who are burdened with heavy
family and work obligations to attempt to write a book or
take on a similarly ambitious project. Practical considera-
tions dictate that we cannot always actualize our creative
ideas, that we must sometimes put them on hold until the
nurturing conditions exist in which they can unfold. At
the same time, however, we must make some time—even
if it is only a few hours a week—for creative expression.
Each of us needs some solitude to tend our "dream
blossoms."

Several clients tell me that although their busy lives preclude ambitious artistic projects, they find that journal writing is an accessible and appropriate outlet for their creative
energies: To keep a journal, one needs only a notebook, a
pen, and short periods of solitude. Yet, despite the minimal
investment, keeping a journal, as the following vignettes
illustrate, can be very healing.

Tina confided that after her divorce, she felt frighten-
ingly alone. "I didn't know anyone in the small city where
my ex-husband and I had recently settled, and I dared not
contact my family. I knew how disapproving my parents
would be about a divorce." In desperation, she began a
personal journal: "I had no one to talk to, so I began to
talk to my journal." Even after Tina eventually remarried
and made new friends, she continued to write in her
journal.

Journaling proved to be a healing and creative outlet. It encourages me to recognize my emotions and find the most descriptive words for them. When I write, I become the patient, accepting mother I never really had, the mother who wipes away her little girl's tears and says, "There, there, honey, it's all right. You can tell me what's wrong. Take your time and tell me all about it." As I take my time to express myself in my journal, I feel calmer. The problems that were monstrous and nameless now seem smaller, more manageable.

One of my dearest clients, eighty-two-year-old Amelia, who initiated therapy in order to come to terms with an estrangement from her middle-aged daughter, also benefited from keeping a journal. Amelia did not take this creative task lightly. On the contrary, she took great pains to find the word or phrase that precisely depicted her feelings and captured the essence of her inner experience.

> I am quite dissatisfied with the terms depression and sadness, my dear Evi, for they do not do justice to my inner state. Ah, but I was delighted to come up with "confused, helpless frustration."
>
> "Anger" is so overused, it has lost its meaning for me. "Raving fury"—now that is rich!
>
> I am writing about my deep feelings for my grandchild but dislike describing myself as her "role model," a term without heart. I was hoping that you would help me find a synonym that is more emotional in tone.

During months of writing in her journal, Amelia developed a lexicon of expressions that depicted her unique feelings and responses to the world, and each time she told me that she had come upon the right word or phrase, Amelia's beautiful face broke into a great smile. As she said, "Sloppy descriptions distort what I am all about, but carefully chosen ones dignify the meanings of my life."

To our mutual delight, Amelia eventually decided that her writing, which was of such personal value, could also enhance others. Her journal has become a life review—a record of Amelia's adventures over eight decades as well as a description of the family members who had an impact on her life. Amelia intends to pass her writings on to her only grandchild so that this little girl will one day know the richness of her roots and thereby enlarge her self-understanding. Amelia still has no contact with her daughter but because she believes she can contribute to the well-being of her daughter's daughter, the wound of estrangement stings less.

As we create, we give our inner world new meaning. By drawing a picture or writing or composing, we validate our subjective experience: make it tangible, real, vivid. Paula's giggle and Amelia's great smile reflect the deep satisfaction of affirming one's own life. Indifference is surely the coldest human response. By virtue of giving our lived experience form, we are no longer indifferent to it; we imbue it with significance. And sometimes—as with Amelia and her grandchild—in recognizing the fullness of our own lives and giving them creative expression, we enrich the lives of others.

Of course, the creative act cannot undo the hurts and humiliations we suffer. Still, it does allow us to transform them. Like nets that have tightened into trampolines, the dark feelings that once trammeled us can now propel us. Let me end this chapter with the lovely passage by Gloria Vanderbilt that introduces the section on healing in *Mothering Ourselves*. Coming to terms with the frivolous childhood mother who could not care for her adequately, Vanderbilt writes of her healing creative transformation.

> Her presence fills my memory and dreams, and what was incomplete between us I have overcome in my work. What was painful and destructive I have made into something of my own, changed the sorrow into something vital and accessible.[16]

# PART IV

# Reconciliations

I look around me in this garden behind my mother's house. It has become a wave of light, an affirmation that rises not only beyond sorrow, but from a sense of wondering joy. I glance quickly at my mother, who has fallen silent, and I watch with disbelief the way the distance between us, and all separation, heals over.

—Kim Chernin
*In My Mother's House*

My mother was dead for five years before I knew that I had loved her very much.

—Lillian Hellman
*An Unfinished Woman: A Memoir*

# CHAPTER 9

# *The Silver Shoes*

"My darling child!" she cried, folding the little girl
in her arms and covering her face with kisses;
"where in the world did you come from?"

"From the Land of Oz," said Dorothy gravely.
"And here is Toto, too. And oh, Aunt Em! I'm so
glad to be home again!"

—L. Frank Baum
*The Wizard of Oz*

It is only after Dorothy of *The Wizard of Oz* becomes
whole and vital that she is able to return to Aunt Em. Similarly, as we wounded daughters heal ourselves, we are often
able to return to our own mother in new ways. No longer
starving for her love (for we are learning to find other sources
of nurturance and self-esteem), we can approach her less
desperately; no longer silently raging (for we are learning to
express our inner hurt), we have a chance of making a
peace—perhaps a friendship—with her. And, although we
will never be able to undo the pain and injustices she inflicted
on us when we were younger, we can work toward a mutually enhancing relationship with her *now*. Even if we discover that mother is too embittered by life or too set in her
ways to meet us halfway, we may find it possible to treat
her fairly and generously.

As small children, we see the world in black and white,
good and bad. This is the main reason that in children's fairy
tales the mother figure, who in reality is a composite of good
and bad, is split into two separate characters: the all-loving
mother and the evil witch. A small child is not fully equipped

to perceive the world in shades of gray, to allow for both bad and good in her mother. But as adults, we have the capacity to tolerate ambivalence; and whether we like it or not, life inevitably teaches us that every human relationship is ambivalent—a mixture of love and hate, comfort and irritation, fulfillment and disappointment. The mother who neglected or abused us, and for this reason deserves our outrage, is also the woman who, wounded herself, deserves our compassion.

Realizing the powers of her Silver Shoes—the symbol of understanding—Dorothy claps the heels together three times and is carried back to Kansas. She discovers that the dismal gray farmhouse, which represents all that was dismal and gray in childhood, has been destroyed by the cyclone; in its place is a shining new structure. In a similar vein, empowered by our greater understanding—knowledge, comprehension, and also empathy—we daughters may be able to restructure our relations with our mothers and to replace what was dismal with something new and shining. In this concluding chapter I try to show daughters how to make this happen.

Throughout this book I have emphasized that the wounded daughter must recognize the ways her mother, by not meeting her natural needs and longings, hurt her. I devoted Chapters 1 through 4 to naming and elaborating the ways mothers often fail the dependent daughter. My intention is not to lash out at mothers, however, but rather to expose the stinging motherwounds so that they might at last heal; covered up, they can only fester. Time and again, in my practice, I have observed the connection between revealing one's deepest hurts and healing one's spirit and, conversely, the connection between covering the motherwound and remaining ill.

For example, thirty-five-year-old Marietta, who had suffered a lifetime of psychosomatic ailments, improved physically after writing a letter to her mother, Helga, in which she articulated pent-up resentments. Putting down on paper the anger she felt against her mother was not easy. Indeed, coming to terms with mother's past injustices at first stimulated more anger as well as confusion, hurt, and guilt. Still, in the long term, expressing her deeply felt emotions allowed Marietta to set them at rest and to find some inner peace.

In contrast, chronically depressed fifty-year-old Laverne refused—even within the safe and confidential setting of therapy—to express outrage at her young mother's irresponsibility for abandoning her when she was an infant. Instead, she found excuses for her mother's behavior while viciously turning against herself: "I'm no good; I'm a bad seed; I should never have been born because I'm just a trouble to everyone."

Until the hurt child within is given a voice, she will clamor for attention—by giving us headaches, irritable bowels, back pains, and bouts of depression and anxiety; or by repeating patterns of abuse against ourselves and others. Understandably, like Laverne, we may resist calling forth our wounded child because we fear she will unloose in us hostile feelings, even rage, toward the mother we have dutifully protected. Yet articulating the pain of the hurt inner child and feeling tenderly toward her are absolutely necessary in the healing process.

What is important to understand, however, and what I focus on in this chapter, is the fact that recognizing and affirming the hurt inner child may not be enough. In addition to developing self-compassion, we must also develop compassion for our mother; if full healing is to occur, we must learn to identify and empathize with her.

When we hold the view that mother is a monster, a fool, or a misfit, we are likely to suspect these character defects in our personalities as well. In contrast, when we are compassionate toward mother, we have a better chance of loving ourselves. As an elementary school teacher in Harlem, I learned that the cruelest insult a child could hurl against another was to say something derogatory about his or her mother. In fact, the mere words "Your mother" were red flags and usually provocation enough for a fist fight. Certainly such insults challenged family loyalty, but I believe my pupils knew intuitively that demeaning remarks against their mother were also attacks on them. However much we protest against this fact, we are our mother's daughter—her life is a part of ours. Jung understood this when he wrote, "Every mother contains her daughter in herself and every daughter her mother, and every woman extends backwards into her mother and forward into her daughter."[1]

In order to know and appreciate ourselves, we must also come to know and appreciate the woman who bore and raised us, and we can best do this by putting ourselves in her place. My client Marietta was able to do this. Months after she wrote her candid letter to Helga, which, not surprisingly, was met by angry silence, Marietta reached out to her. As she told me, "Now that I felt stronger and healthier, I was ready to meet my mother and to try to understand her life *from her point of view*."

A wise saying of the American Indian counsels us to refrain from criticizing a brother until we have walked a mile in his moccasins. Let us also recall that as Dorothy is about to embark on the yellow brick road toward recovery, the good Witch of the North commands her to walk in the Silver Shoes that belonged to the wicked Witch of the East.

Personal histories vary, of course, but most of our mothers were shaped by cultures that limited and demeaned women. Understanding how our wounding mothers were themselves wounded can put into better perspective their maternal shortcomings. When, for example, I recognize that my bright, energetic grandmother was turned away from medical school simply because she was a woman, I am less likely to think badly of her for expressing disappointment that she bore only daughters and for rejecting her last-born baby girl—who, she anticipated, would also be prevented from pursuing her ambitions. When I accept the fact that my mother's most powerful tool was her good looks, I can understand why she placed more meaning on my appearance than on the drawings, short stories, and impressive school grades I offered up to her for loving approval. And when I become increasingly aware of the widespread propaganda of the late forties, fifties, and early sixties—magazine articles, novels, "expert" advice—that equated a woman's decency and success only with her status as gracious homemaker, I can appreciate my mother's lack of support when I first told her I had decided to go to graduate school and that my husband would shoulder the lion's share of housework and childcare for a time.

Reflecting on the limited lives of women, I am reminded of Jack Clayton's movie *The Lonely Passion of Judith Hearne*. In the opening scene, which is a flashback, a happy, radiant child sits in a church pew next to a stern and imperious elderly woman. When, during the service, the little girl begins to giggle, the forbidding caretaker restrains her by fiercely squeezing her hand. As the movie camera shifts from the wrinkled old hand with the tender young one in its grip to the child's pained expression, one cannot help but know that life-joy is being squeezed out of young Judith; and, indeed, on the screen, the image of the innocent little girl dissolves into the tense middle-aged face of Miss Judith Hearne.

The conditions of our mothers' times often squeezed the joy of possibility out of them. The lessons they learned too well were to shrivel their own talents and minimize their ambitions. That they would also inhibit the lives of their daughters, with whom they identified most strongly, becomes understandable.

When, as a young child growing up in the fifties, I was sick enough to stay home from school, I used to watch the daytime TV program "Queen for a Day." As many readers of my generation may remember, the female contestants on this show related their woeful life conditions. By their applause, the audience would judge who was the most miserable and pitiful of the lot, and she became queen for a day! Is it any wonder that some of our mothers have difficulty encouraging our success when they were prized for their suffering? Is it not also understandable that some of our mothers, disallowed from realizing their potential, alternately envy or try to live through us?

In her letter, Marietta justifiably took issue with her mother, Helga, for being intrusive, domineering, and controlling. During college, for example, Helga planned her daughter's course schedules and even chose her major for her. Moreover, Helga was never too ashamed to open the envelope—addressed to Marietta!—that contained a transcript of her final grades. It was healthy for Marietta to confront her mother for these abuses of power but, as she explained, it also became necessary to understand the reasons for her mother's behavior.

> After I had vented my long overdue anger and calmed down enough to talk honestly with my mother, I discovered that she wasn't the monster I had made her out to be. I realized that she was a very smart lady who never had an outlet for her intellect. As a young woman, she didn't have an opportunity to go to college, and, after she married, my father wouldn't let her take a job outside the home and even discouraged her from doing volunteer work. Being a housewife was not challenging enough for this bright, imaginative woman. So, she lived through me. Of course, it was wrong of her to do this to me. But I can understand her reasons. It all makes sense.

Going directly to our mothers for information about their lives, as Marietta did, enlarges our understanding. We can also look elsewhere for our Silver Shoes. Classics such as Simone de Beauvoir's *The Second Sex*, Betty Friedan's *The Feminine Mystique*, Adrienne Rich's *Of Woman Born*, and Jesse Bernard's *The Future of Motherhood* can also teach us. Feminist scholars have done us a wonderful service in providing a compelling literature that documents the victimization of women by sexism in the past. Treated like cute Christmas tree ornaments or, alternately, abused as sex objects, is it any wonder that so many of our mothers never developed a healthy sense of selfhood and, as a consequence, failed to affirm us?

Knowing how our grandmothers and mothers were hurt cannot undo or excuse the hurt they may have in turn caused us—what de Beauvoir calls "the chain of female misery"—but it can at least provide explanations for their inadequacies. Instead of perceiving maternal failings wholly as personal defects, we can try to understand them as outgrowths of a society that generally stunted women; instead of seeing our mothers as monsters, fools, or misfits, we can look upon them as victims of their times. Thus, like Dorothy of *The Wizard of Oz*, by virtue of the powers of our Silver Shoes—our understanding—we can *melt* the image of the witch-mother.

It is noteworthy that in the movie version of *The Wizard of Oz*, Dorothy's melting of the wicked Witch is a violent act: an annihilation. But melting also softens and makes someone gentle and tender. When our mothers know that we are trying to understand rather than evaluate them, they are likely to "melt"—to become less rigid, stubborn, and defensive. Similarly, as we make efforts to recognize the truth of their lives—to appreciate their struggles and limitations, as well as their triumphs—our long-held resentments may begin to melt away.

In therapy, I suggest several ways for women to develop a deeper understanding of their mothers' life circumstances. For example, I may ask a client to imagine that she is her mother and, speaking from the older woman's perspective, tell her life story. By stepping into mother's shoes, the adult daughter often feels a new tenderness for her. One of my clients, Tanya, told me that when she assumed her mother's character—taking on her voice, facial expression, and posture—she could feel mother shrink from a tyrannical presence to an insecure, bewildered little person. Then, rather than being afraid of her, she felt a certain sympathy.

When I role-play my mother, I can actually feel how her rigidity and control are the ways she defends against falling apart. Stepping into her shoes, it's hard to be intimidated any longer because I experience her as lacking confidence, not just mean and hurtful.

Sometimes I suggest to my clients that they become "students of behavior" and puzzle out why their mothers act as they do. Recently, I took my own advice. I had felt hurt and ignored because in weekly phone conversations with my mother, she talked enthusiastically about her activities but seemed uninterested in the details of my family's life. Although she would ask, "How is Bruce's health?" or "Are you working too hard?" or "Are Leah and Jonathan happy in school?" she never let me answer but jumped in to tell me, "It's wonderful that you're all doing so well." And when I did manage to let her know that all was not rosy, she seemed to minimize my concerns or not to hear me at all. Putting myself in her place, I suddenly understood that my mother, who loves us dearly, wants to believe that we are happy and healthy. Having struggled against poverty, religious persecution, and the myriad losses intrinsic to every long life, she now wants peace of mind rather than reports of her children's troubles and woes.[2]

Sometimes I recommend that a client write a biography of her mother. Such an ambitious project involves researching the mother's life, which can turn up all sorts of surprises. One client, Shirley, had always felt embarrassed by her Hungarian mother for her old-fashioned, foreign ways. ("When I had to go shopping with her, I stayed far enough away so that people would not think I belonged to this loud, pushy woman with the thick European accent.") For her part, Shirley's mother, Elsa, made little effort to understand and respect the world of her American-born child. ("My mother never had a nice word to say about my friends, my teachers, or *me*.") Each sensing the other's rejection and lack of empathy, Shirley and Elsa grew increasingly distant over the years. Although they now lived in commuting distance of one another, their relationship consisted of the exchange of birthday cards and encounters at family weddings or funerals.

When Shirley approached her mother for an "interview," Elsa was shocked but also touched by her daughter's sudden interest in her life. Excitedly spreading out old letters and yellowed newspaper clippings on the kitchen table, she shared her life story with her daughter for the first time. And now, instead of shame, Shirley felt proud of her mother—this loud, pushy woman who, by dint of will as strong as steel, had cut through mounds of red tape to leave her repressive homeland and emigrate to America alone when she was barely nineteen. Not surprisingly, in the process of getting to like her mother better, Shirley also became more self-accepting—more tolerant of her own stubborn and sometimes hypercritical nature.

Unlike Shirley, other wounded daughters, despite conscientious efforts, may not be able to discover admirable qualities in their mothers. In these cases, I sometimes suggest making a connection with the little girl mother once was. To this end, I have asked clients to bring in photographs of mother when she was very young.

Josie, the daughter of a multiple drug user who refuses treatment, was brought up by aunts and a grandmother. With justification, Josie had felt only disgust toward her mother: "How can I feel anything positive for this woman whose single concern in life is to get her next fix?" But when Josie and I leafed through old family albums and saw photos of Josie's mother as a child, she softened and was able to feel tenderness for this sweet-faced little girl. As Josie put it, "My mother is not the devil. She is not 'Rosemary's Baby,' but just an innocent child who grew up to become terribly damaged."

Wounded adult daughters are sometimes afraid of extending empathy to their mothers. They fear that by approaching mother with a soft heart and by feeling compassion for her, they will not longer have a right to be angry at her for earlier or present injustices. They assume that in feeling sorry for her, they will be compelled to forgive her and to forget their own suffering. But they are mistaken: Developing compassion for the wounded mother does not preclude honoring the pain of the hurt child within oneself.

In recent years, a slew of experts have written about the relationship between parents and wounded adult children. Although they often provide valuable insights, they also tend to depict relationships in absolute terms. Some counsel us not to hold mother accountable for her wrongs but instead to direct all our anger at the patriarchal society that victimizes women; at the other extreme, some debunk the adult child's hope of making any meaningful connection with "dysfunctional" parents. To my mind, these solutions are over simplified and inadequate. As I see it, true healing is a more complicated process that entails eight steps.

(1) Recognizing that our mothers have wounded us;

(2) Understanding the nature of these wounds;

(3) Expressing our legitimate hurt or outrage;

(4) Finding ways to soothe our pain;

(5) Finding creative ways to transform our pain;

(6) Trying not to repeat old destructive patterns;

(7) Extending empathy to the wounding mother; and

(8) Trying to restructure the present mother–adult daughter relationship.

The overwhelming majority of people are not permanently "dysfunctional" but are capable of positive change throughout the life cycle. In most cases, the inadequate mother of our childhood can evolve into the "good enough" mother (and grandmother) of our adulthood. To be sure, a small number of mothers—Josie's chronically drug-addicted mother is one example, the incesting or sadistic or blatantly narcissistic mother another—function at such primitive levels that a positive human relationship may not be possible. In such situations, a daughter may have no choice but to sever the attachment. Cutting physical ties with our mother is an extreme and tragic solution, but it is preferable to being in a relationship that continually harms us. Each of us has but one life and our first responsibility is to take precious care of it. We cannot allow another person—even our own mother—to destroy us.

Even if the only solution is to physically distance ourselves from the ever-wounding mother, coming to understand (as Josie did) that mother was not born a monster will enable us to accept ourselves. I am reminded of the touching story of a young male client, which, although it regards the father-son relationship, may help some of my female readers.

David, a charming and highly successful college student, initiated therapy in order to make sense of a tormented relationship with his insensitive, neglectful, "good-for-nothing" father—a man who had emotionally and financially abandoned his wife and four children. Although David wanted to identify with him, he was not able to discover anything sympathetic, let alone admirable, about this unloving man. Forlorn and increasingly embittered, David resolved to drop his surname as a way of renouncing any tie with the noxious father: "The truth is that I have nothing in common with this man who *happens* to have fathered me. In our values, in our personalities, we are opposites. It's ridiculous that a family name should bind us." Before David took this radical action, however, I suggested that he explore the concept that every human being is both light and shadow, both good and bad.

A week later, David came to therapy in an ebullient mood. To my surprise, he announced that he would not drop his last name because he had found a meaningful connection with his father after all. As David explained, it was not their likenesses but rather their dissimilarities that bound them. Empathic, generous, and capable of relationship, David concluded that he was living out what his incomplete, deficient father could not; he was the light and the good that had remained hidden in the older man. Now father and son had become a unity of sorts, and, although David understood that an in-the-flesh relationship would never be possible (for David's father remained cold, uninvolved, and undermining), he could maintain a spiritual connection that made him feel less lost and abandoned.

Time and again, my clients teach me that there are unconventional ways to heal the wounds of childhood and make peace with our parents. In the previous chapter, I described Paula's ability to lift herself out of her depression through her art work. In spite of her creative success, however, Paula was saddened by the fact that she could not achieve a satisfactory relationship with her mother. Whenever they were together, the old woman undermined Paula by harshly criticizing the way she lived. She also verbally attacked Paula's husband and children, who began to dread Granny's visits, and, although Paula implored her mother to be more affirming, she continued to be unkind. After much consideration, Paula decided to put an end to their contacts—a decision that caused her much sorrow.

Recently, Paula took a part-time position as a practical nurse in a hospital and discovered that she is especially drawn to elderly patients. In fact, Paula has developed an affection for the cranky, critical, and cantankerous old women whom the other nurses find insufferable. Although it is too "dangerous" for Paula to allow a closeness with her own mother, she is able to express a tender, compassionate, filial care for these surrogate mothers who do not pose a personal threat to her. In this indirect way, Paula has become the loving and devoted "daughter" she could not be with her own mother.

In contrast to Josie, David, and Paula, most adult children can develop a vital relationship with their real parents. One of the keys to healthy relationship is honest communication. However, in counseling mothers and adult daughters, I am struck by the fact that all too frequently they do not talk to each other in any meaningful way.

For example, adult daughters often believe that they must

walk on eggshells around their mothers and do not trust that they can safely disagree. I once counseled a tiny woman, thin as a rail and barely five feet tall, who thought nothing of confronting her burly husband when he displeased her. However, at my suggestion that she take a firm stand with her mother, who was making outrageous demands on her time, she insisted, "Oh, I could never do *that!*"

For many adult daughers, opposing or denying mother feels dangerous because at some deep level we still believe that she may withdraw her love from us if we get her angry. As my client Tanya told me when she first began therapy, "If I dare say no to my elderly mother, who is a very cranky and demanding lady, I am convinced that either she or I will die." Although in her mid-forties, Tanya held the child's view that failure to comply absolutely with mother's needs or wishes leads to terrible punishment. Better to muffle herself than to say anything to incur mother's wrath. Yet if we hope to achieve adult-to-adult friendships with our mothers, we must learn to talk to them—openly, directly, sometimes firmly.

A few years ago, during a phone conversation, my mother, who is a widow with modest means, told me how comforting it was for her to know that I would always be there to take care of her and that, for this reason, she never concerned herself about the problems of old age. Although I agreed that she could depend on me for emotional and financial support, I felt vaguely irritated by her remark—a feeling that did not pass but rather grew into an oppressive resentment over the next months. Slowly, I was able to admit to myself that I dreaded taking responsibility for my mother; but for a long time I dared not share this sentiment with another soul for fear of being thought a selfish and disloyal daughter. When I finally brought up my "shameful" secret with my friend Susan, she legitimized my feelings and helped me articulate them: To be held solely responsible for someone else's welfare seemed an unfair burden. I wanted my mother to take *reasonable* control of her own future.

After my friend had helped me define my problem, I was

faced with the matter of bringing it up to my mother. Like Tanya, I worried that if I denied my mother full devotion, either she or I would surely die—or at least fall apart. With a pounding heart and trembling hands, I called my mother and told her that I felt overwhelmed by the prospect of being responsible for her. I explained that although I wanted always to be of some support, I did not have the emotional or financial resources to become her full support.

When I presented my problem in this way I discovered that my mother did not die from grief or shock at my "disloyalty," nor did she fall apart. Instead, *she rallied*. (Our real mother is usually much more resilient and reasonable than the mother we have invented!) Although she was at first taken aback by my pronouncement, within a couple of weeks after our telephone conversation, my mother got information about programs and benefits for the elderly, and together we came up with, if not perfect solutions, possible options for her future. Moreover, she told me that she was happy that I could be honest with her. With the weight of resentment lifted, I felt renewed love and respect for my mother.

Certainly not all problems lead to tangible solutions such as ours. But as the following vignette illustrates, talking things out often dissolves the barriers between mothers and daughters. During the course of therapy, Louise became determined to tell her mother how her earlier abuse—beatings and cruel words—had hurt her. Until she let go the burden of accumulated bitterness toward her mother, Louise doubted that she could ever fully heal and that they could become friends.

As it turned out, Louise's mother was able to listen to her daughter. And although she could not take back the beatings and cruel words, she was now able to say, "I'm sorry that I was not a kind mother to you." With this simple apology, Louise's mother, who had grown and mellowed over the years, affirmed the legitimacy of her daughter's long-felt resentment against her. Louise, in turn, could begin to let it go. (I think we can be very helpful to our mothers when we explain to them that we are not asking that they fix past mistakes—which, after all, is impossible to do—but rather that they simply recognize them.)

Language is a powerful tool. As we learn better ways to speak to our mothers, we make it possible for us to become friends with them. If we can present our differences and grievances in a clear, calm, firm but nonabusive way, they are likely to take them seriously and accommodate us. In contrast, if we blame, attack, or humiliate them, they will defend themselves by denying, withdrawing, or counterattacking, and we will end up frustrated and in despair.

Building a healthier relationship with our aging mothers also entails redefining our expectations of them as parents and of ourselves as daughters. Before Dorothy can return to Aunt Em, she must remove her green-tinted glasses and see the world in its true colors. Similarly, as we adult daughters return to our mothers, we must remove the veils from our eyes to see clearly.

In a sense, every daughter harbors two mothers: the human, limited, imperfect mother and the ideal Mother, who is always supportive, approving, empathic, wise, and infinitely loving. As small children, we insisted that our mother was perfect because, helpless and dependent, we relied on her beneficence absolutely. Moreover, basking in the glow of her imagined perfection, we could feel wonderful and special too. When as adults, however, we continue to expect our human mother to take the role of her godly counterpart, the magic Mother, we are bound to feel deceived—much as Dorothy feels duped after discovering that the Wizard is at best an ordinary little person. And just as the Wizard proclaims, "How can I help being a humbug . . . when all these people make me do things that everybody knows can't be done?"[3] our real mother, who is necessarily unable to measure up to our idealized versions of her, may feel like a humbug—an imposter—too.

The adult daughter must both recognize mother's real parental failures *and* identify unrealistic expectations of her.

Certainly, it is not easy to relinquish the wish for the all-loving, all-knowing Mother, for she promises infinite happiness. But give it up we must if we are ever to make a viable relationship with our human mother and become strong ourselves. Mimi, one of my clients, shared the following experience.

When my sixty-year-old mother was diagnosed with terminal cancer, I realized that I was very angry at her. I even avoided visiting her as often as I should have, and I convinced myself that she was somehow responsible for getting sick. I understand now that the child in me expected my mother to be there forever. She was to remain young, beautiful, and healthy. It has taken me a long time to come to terms with my mortal mother, who must leave me now.

Another client, Lee, confided a similar sentiment.

The Mother I wished for—and had insisted my mother become—was to be my wisest teacher, so that by taking her counsel I could not help but follow the right path. My real mother, however, cannot guide my way because she is not well educated or insightful. For many years I was angry at my mother because she did not have the answers. She was not the intelligent mother I thought I deserved. What I understand now is that the teacher I looked for in her, I must find elsewhere.

Paradoxically, the maternal limitations that disappoint and enrage us can also push our growth. If Aunt Em had been all-fulfilling, Dorothy would not have ventured into the wonderful world of Oz; if our mothers were infinitely loving, wise, and available, we would never want to grow up and leave them. Deprived of the desired mentor-mother, for example, Lee searched for old, wise women. She made friends with a housebound eighty-year-old British lady who had been a writer and university professor, and she visited her weekly: "We have animated conversations about literature, world affairs, and so many other things. And Mrs. Martin, my old friend, sweetens our intellectual discussions with pots of hot tea and home-made scones," Lee says.

Despite her great affection for the woman, Lee was also able to acknowledge Mrs. Martin's limitations. Mrs. Martin admitted she had not done well with her children. She had been, she told Lee, a natural woman of letters but an unnatural mother who tried to "mix ink and mothermilk" and made a mess of things on the home front. No, Mrs. Martin was not the lost primordial goddess-mother of Lee's longings. Rather, she was a very human mother-figure, with strengths and weaknesses, who provided the intellectual guidance that Lee's mother could not.

Building a better relationship with our mothers requires that, in addition to accepting their human limitations, we recognize our own limitations as daughters. Just as we must relinquish the childish ideal of the all-fulfilling mother—for she is lost to us forever—we must relinquish the ideal of the all-fulfilling daughter. It is a paradox that as children, although we feel small and helpless, we also attribute enormous (illusory) power to ourselves: the power to make our mothers happy or sad, healthy or sick. In adulthood, we come to terms with our limitations, including the fact that we cannot fill our mothers' needs and that they, not we, are responsible for creating their own meanings and happiness. Nevertheless, knowing that our mother's life is not and perhaps never was full enough necessarily weighs heavily.

As emotionally difficult as accepting the less-than-happy condition of mother's life is *choosing* not to give as much care and attention as she may ask for in her old age. When mother becomes frail and increasingly dependent on others, each of us will decide what our commitment to her is and what it is not—when to say yes and when to say no. For some, meeting our elderly mother's physical and emotional needs is an affirmation of strong family ties, a source of pride and renewed tenderness. For others, however, it may become an unbearable burden. "I am alternately so sad about my mother's decline that I can't stop crying and so enraged that my life is being messed up that I want to dump her. I used to think I was good at crises, but this just goes on and on, and I'm falling apart," says a middle-aged daughter in an interview for the *New York Times*.[4]

Deciding what is reasonable care for the elderly parent and what are unreasonable sacrifices is a complex, individual, and often heart-wrenching decision. If, *after careful consideration*, we chose not to give mother as much as she would like, we are wise to refrain from wallowing in guilt; we should rather remind ourselves of our limitations. Like mothers, daughters are not infinite sources of nurturance.

In *Mothers and Daughters: Loving and Letting Go*, I tell a story attributed to Freud that is worth repeating here. During a great flood, an eagle is about to carry her three newborns to dry ground. As she takes flight, clutching her firstborn in her mighty talons, he promises, "Mother, I will be eternally grateful and devoted to you for saving my life." Naming him a liar, she drops the eaglet into the raging waters below. The same thing happens with the second. When the great eagle sweeps up the third, this offspring says, "When I am grown, I will try to be as good a parent to my young ones as you are to me," and her mother carries her to safety.[5] Between mother and child, there can never be a quid pro quo. As the wise eaglet reminds us, the debt of gratitude we owe our mothers for nurturing us will not be paid back to them directly or in full. If our mothers express resentment because we are not devoted enough, it may be reassuring to remind them that their precious gift of motherlove enables us to become "good enough" parents to our own children or, if we are childless, to contribute in our own creative ways to the generation that follows us.

It is a wonderful relief when we can let go the expectation of perfection—perfection in our mothers, perfection in ourselves—when we no longer insist that our mothers or we do things for each other that cannot be done. Accepting our mutual human ordinariness, mothers and daughters can return to one another with new understanding.

*     *     *

Having made the journey across the Land of Oz, which, as the good Witch of the North promised, was "sometimes pleasant and sometimes dark and terrible," Dorothy, empowered by new understanding, is ready to return to the real world and the less-than-happy family she left behind.[6] After she claps the heels of her shoes together three times and calls out, "Take me home to Aunt Em!" a great gust whirls her through the air and carries her back to the broad Kansas prairie. Looking about her in amazement, Dorothy discovers that she is on the grass in front of the new farmhouse Uncle Henry built after the cyclone carried away the old one.

> Uncle Henry was milking the cows in the barnyard, and Toto had jumped out of her arms and was running toward the barn, barking joyously. . . .
> Aunt Em had just come out of the house to water the cabbages when she looked up and saw Dorothy running toward her.
> "My darling child!" she cried, folding the little girl in her arms and covering her face with kisses; "where in the world did you come from?"
> "From the Land of Oz," said Dorothy gravely. "And here is Toto, too. And oh, Aunt Em! I'm so glad to be home again!"[7]

It is an ordinary Saturday morning in Boulder, the day my mother expects me to call her. In the past I have not been good about these calls: Sometimes I have put them off until late afternoon, sometimes I have "forgotten" them all together. When we do talk, I am often irritated because she is not attuned to me; our conversations are strained and unsatisfying. But this morning I want to hear my mother's voice. My eagerness surprises me, and I do not stop to question it.

I quickly push the buttons on the receiver and she answers after half a ring, "Oh, Evi, darling, I knew it would be you even before the telephone rang." She asks about the family but does not wait to hear that this has been an especially difficult week for us. Instead, she tells me about herself. I could easily become indignant at her for cutting me off; I could turn into stone. But I *decide* to let go of my anger. My heart softens and opens up to her: I smile as she tells me about the good weather they are having in Florida and the wonderful all-day cruise that she and her new companion, John, have just taken.

As my mother goes on talking about her activities to the exclusion of mine, I am aware of the way she distances herself emotionally by tuning me out, but right now I can accept her shortcomings; they do not sting me. In fact, listening to my mother bubble over, I cannot help but enjoy her, and I think to myself that when I too am old, I will try to be as enthusiastic as she is—to relish life's simple pleasures, whether these are a few mild, sunny days or a boat ride that goes nowhere in particular.

The conversation winds down; we say goodbye. But just before she hangs up, I tell her that Bruce, the children, and I are happy and healthy.

"Wonderful," she says without asking for details. "That is the news that I love so much to hear. You can be sure I will sleep well tonight!"

"I understand," I reply. "That's why I'm telling you."

I look down at my feet. At this moment my Silver Shoes are shining ever so brightly.

# NOTES AND ELABORATIONS

## Introduction

1. Louise Bernikow, *Among Women* (New York: Harper & Row, 1981), p. 47.
2. Tillie Olsen, "Tell Me a Riddle," *Tell Me a Riddle* (New York: Dell, 1960), p. 107.
3. W. H. Auden, quoted by Emanuel H. Hammer in "Artistic Creativity: Giftedness or Sickness." *The Arts in Psychotherapy*, vol. 2 (1975), p. 175.
4. To protect my clients' rights of confidentiality, I have disguised their identities by changing the details of their situations. In several cases, I have combined the histories of two or more clients to form composites.

## Chapter 1

1. Heinz Kohut, *How Does Analysis Cure?* (Chicago: University of Chicago Press, 1984), p. 143. Heinz Kohut's conception is elaborated by Anthony Storr in *Solitude: A Return to the Self* (New York: Free Press, 1988): "A clear, clean polished mirror will repeatedly reflect the developing person as he actually is, and thus give him a firm and true sense of his own identity. A cracked, dirty, smeared mirror will reflect an incomplete, obscured image which provides the child with an inaccurate and distorted picture of himself" (p. 149). Hence, the psychologically healthy parent is able to recognize or mirror the child in a way that the unhealthy parent cannot.
2. Daniel N. Stern, *The Interpersonal World of the Infant* (New York: Basic Books, 1985), p. 196.
3. Kohut contends that the most severe form of anxiety is "disintegration anxiety." In the absence of empathic parental responses during childhood, the individual does not develop a strong, coherent sense of self and, when under stress, will feel in danger of falling apart.

4. Vivian Gornick, *Fierce Attachments* (New York: Simon & Schuster, 1987), pp. 103–104.
5. Toni Morrison, *Beloved* (New York: New American Library, 1987), p. 243.
6. Readers interested in a comprehensive treatment from a Jungian perspective of the Narcissus myth are referred to Nathan Schwartz-Salant's *Narcissism and Character Transformation* (Toronto: Inner City Books, 1982).
7. Quoted in ibid., p. 95.
8. Richard A. Geist, "Therapeutic Dilemmas in the Treatment of Anorexia Nervosa: A Self-Psychological Perspective," *Theory and Treatment of Anorexia and Bulimia*, edited by S. W. Emmett (New York: Brunner/Mazel, 1985), p. 272.
9. Th. Christiansen Reidar, ed., "Mophead," *Folktales of Norway* (Chicago: University of Chicago Press, 1964), pp. 252–258. The story of Mophead is known in Sweden, Iceland, and Ireland; some variants are also reported from southeast European and Anglo-American traditions.
10. From Alphonse Daudet's *Lettres de Mon Moulin* (Paris: Nelson, Éditeurs) retold by Alice Miller, *The Drama of the Gifted Child* (New York: Basic Books, 1981), pp. 28–29.

## Chapter 2

1. Bruce Bassoff, *Back Through the Glass* (© Bruce Bassoff, 1988), p. 30.
2. Ibid., p. 31.
3. Ibid.
4. Marlo Thomas, *Free to be . . . you and me* (New York: McGraw Hill, 1974).
5. Mary McCarthy, *The Group* (New York: Harcourt, Brace, and World, 1954), p. 345.
6. Mary Klinnert, Joseph Campos, and Robert Emde, "The Role of Maternal Facial Signaling on the Visual Cliff," *Developmental Psychology*, vol. 21 (1985), pp. 195–200.
7. Virginia Woolf, "Professions for Women," cited in Karen Payne, ed., *Between Ourselves: Letters Between Mothers and Daughters* (Boston: Houghton Mifflin, 1983), p. 3.
8. Alice Miller, *The Drama of the Gifted Child* (New York: Basic Books, 1981), p. 47.
9. Alice Munro, "Red Dress," *Dance of the Happy Shades* (New York: McGraw Hill, 1968), p. 160.
10. Miller, *The Drama of the Gifted Child*, p. 13.
11. Louise Bernikow, *Among Women* (New York: Harper & Row, 1981), p. 64.

12. Colette, *My Mother's House and Sido* (New York: Farrar, Straus and Giroux, 1953), p. 13.
13. Maurice Goudeket, *Close to Colette* (New York: Farrar, Straus and Giroux, 1957), p. 31.

**Chapter 3**

1. Hillel, cited in Martin Buber, *I and Thou* (New York: Scribner, 1970), p. 85.
2. The enhancing mother of the infant or young child, who is necessarily dependent and relatively helpless, is responsive to the child's great needs for physical care and emotional comfort; she is willing to put the baby's needs for nurturance before her own. As the child grows and develops, the enhancing mother modifies her caretaking role and encourages the child's age-appropriate independence and respect for others—including respect for her. Over time, the healthy mother-child relationship fosters a dual recognition, whereby each recognizes and honors one's own individual needs as well as the rights of the other. See Jessica Benjamin, *The Bonds of Love: Psychoanalysis, Feminism, and the Problem of Domination* (New York: Pantheon, 1988), Chapter One; and Evelyn Bassoff, *Mothers and Daughters: Loving and Letting Go* (New York: New American Library, 1988) for further discussion.
3. John Thor Dahlburg (Associated Press), *Boulder Daily Camera*, December 29, 1988, section 1, p. 1.
4. Bruno Bettelheim, *The Uses of Enchantment* (New York: Vintage Books, 1977), p. 146. Bettelheim points out that a human's greatest fear is abandonment—separation anxiety—and the younger we are, the more excruciating is this fear, for the young child actually perishes when not adequately protected or cared for. Therefore, the ultimate consolation is that we shall never be deserted; this is the theme of the cycle of Iskender tales.
5. Research in the field of neurobiology suggests the profound psychobiological affects of the mother-infant bond. There is evidence that the mother serves as a mediator of soothing and arousal in the child and that these maternal functions have long-term effects. For example, the mother's stroking and holding appears to stimulate the development of opiate receptors in the infant's brain. Unresponsive or abusive caretakers may inhibit the child's ability to modulate strong emotions and to self-soothe. For a review of the interactions between maternal attachment and neurobiological development in the child, readers are referred to Bessel A. van der Kolk, "The Trauma Spec-

trum: The Interaction of Biological and Social Events in the Genesis of the Trauma Response," *Journal of Traumatic Stress*, vol. 1, no. 3 (1988), pp. 273–290.

6. Colette, *My Mother's House and Sido* (New York: Farrar, Straus and Giroux, 1953), p. 29.
7. Ibid., p. 115.
8. Ibid., p. 25.
9. Ibid., p. 5.
10. Gloria Steinem, "Ruth's Song (Because She Could Not Sing It)," *Outrageous Acts and Everyday Rebellions* (New York: Holt, Rinehart & Winston, 1983), p. 146.
11. Tillie Olsen, *Tell Me a Riddle* (New York: Dell, 1960), pp. 2–3.
12. There is some research evidence that self-destructive activities such as self-mutilation, alcohol and drug abuse, and eating disorders are not primarily related to conflict and guilt, but to more primitive biologically based behavior patterns originating in painful encounters with hostile caretakers during the first years of life. See van der Kolk, "The Trauma Spectrum," pp. 390–391.
13. Heinrich Zimmer, *The King and the Corpse*, edited by Joseph Campbell (New York: Pantheon, 1948), pp. 203–235.
14. In recent years, there has been an upsurge of interest among women in rediscovering the ancient religions of the Mother Goddess. Maintaining that the human mother can rarely meet the expectations of her daughter, Kathie Carlson, author of *In Her Image: The Unhealed Daughter's Search for Her Mother* (Boston: Shambala, 1989), argues effectively for consciously forming a relationship with the archetypal mother or feminine deity. Similarly, Kim Chernin, *Reinventing Eve: Modern Woman in Search of Herself* (New York: Harper & Row, 1988) and Merlin Stone, *Ancient Mirrors of Womanhood* (Boston: Beacon, 1979) and *When God Was a Woman* (New York: Harcourt Brace Jovanovich, 1978) explore the possibilities of identification with ancient goddesses and other heroines.
15. See Judith Lewis Herman, with Lisa Hirschman, *Father-Daughter Incest* (Cambridge: Harvard University Press, 1981), pp. 36–49, for a discussion of the relationship between maternal behavior and father-daughter incest.
16. Ibid., pp. 1–3.
17. Louise DeSalvo, *Virginia Woolf: The Impact of Childhood Sexual Abuse on Her Life and Work* (Boston: Beacon, 1989), supports Alice Miller's position: "The consequences of sexual abuse permeate one's entire life and undermine and contaminate the most fundamental of life's experiences: the formation of one's sense of integrity and worth as a human being" (p. 6).

18. Ibid., p. 104.
19. Virginia Woolf, "A Sketch of the Past,"cited in Susan Cahill, ed., *Mothers, Memories, Dreams and Reflections by Literary Daughters* (New York: New American Library, 1988), p. 317.
20. Ibid.
21. Herman, *Father-Daughter Incest*, p. 44.
22. Cited in DeSalvo, *Virginia Woolf*, p. 140.
23. Ibid., p. 15.
24. Ibid., p. 131.
25. Retold in Irvin D. Yalom, *The Theory and Practice of Group Psychotherapy* (New York: Basic Books, 1975), p. 12.

## Chapter 4

1. Erich Hackl, *Aurora's Motive: A Novel* (New York: Knopf, 1989), p. 43.
2. Brothers Grimm, *Grimm's Fairy Tales* (New York: Grosset & Dunlap, 1945), p. 133.
3. J. A. Simpson, ed., *The Concise Oxford Dictionary of Proverbs* (Oxford and New York: Oxford University Press, 1982), traces this proverb back to 1670 (J. Ray, *Collection of English Proverbs*, Cambridge): "My son's my son, till he hath got him a wife, but my daughter's my daughter all days of her life."
4. The relation between achieving separation from the mother and forming other attachments with women is elaborated in Luise Eichenbaum and Susie Orbach's *Between Women* (New York: Viking, 1988), pp. 56–64.
5. Vivian Gornick, *Fierce Attachments* (New York: Simon & Schuster, 1987), pp. 79–80.
6. Maurice Sendak, *Outside Over There* (New York: Harper & Row, 1981).
7. I am not implying that mothers pull their daughters backward and fathers push them forward, for the most enhancing mothers become role models who point their daughters in new directions; moreover, mothers as well as fathers are often adventurous. Nevertheless—at least when their children are young—mothers *tend* to take a more active role in caretaking and fathers *tend* to take a more active role in play. (See Ross D. Parke and Barbara R. Tinsley, "The Father's Role in Infancy: Determinants of Involvement in Caregiving and Play," *The Role of the Father in Child Development*, edited by Michael E. Lamb [New York: Wiley, 1981], pp. 429–457.) To my mind, such distinctive parental roles are not inherently undesirable but can be complementary.
8. Gornick, *Fierce Attachments*, p. 79.

9. The issue of single-parenting by choice is complicated. It is imperative that women considering this alternative undergo counseling with an informed counselor to ensure their full understanding of the effects of father absence. Moreover, it is most important that mother and child will not be totally dependent on each other but will have other loving people to whom to turn for support and refuge.

10. Olive Schreiner, "From Three Dreams in a Desert," *A Track to the Water's Edge: The Olive Schreiner Reader*, edited by Howard Thurman (New York: Harper & Row, 1973), pp. 54–55.

## Chapter 5

1. I would like to express my gratitude to Betsy Hitchcock for pointing me to *The Wizard of Oz*. First written in 1900, the book was made into a movie in 1939, which starred Judy Garland.

2. L. Frank Baum, *The Wizard of Oz* (New York: Ballantine Books, 1979, first printing by Contemporary Books, 1956), p. 2.

3. Ibid., p. 10.

4. Ibid., p. 33.

5. Ibid., p. 13.

6. On a recent trip to Greece, it became clear to me that Dorothy's journey along the yellow brick road to encounter the Wizard parallels the pilgrimage of the ancient Greeks along the Sacred Way to Delphi and the oracle of Apollo—the god of psychological and spiritual insight and healing. Like Dorothy, who expects the magnificent Wizard to solve her problems, the ancient Athenians looked to the god Apollo for guidance and wisdom.

    While we can never know exactly what kind of counsel the oracle of Apollo provided, for the rituals at Delphi were veiled in mystery, we can assume that for the Athenians the long journey to Delphi was as healing as the actual encounter with the oracle. Rollo May writes in *The Courage to Create* (New York: Norton, 1975): "An Athenian setting out on a trip to Delphi to consult Apollo would be turning over in his imagination at almost every moment in the journey this figure of light and healing. Spinoza adjured us to fix our attention on a desired virtue, and we would thus tend to acquire it. Our Greek would be doing this on his trip, and the psychological processes of anticipation, hope, and faith would already be at work. Thus he would be proleptically participating in his own 'cure' " (pp. 98–99). Similarly, on her travels along the yellow brick road to Emerald City where the powerful Oz resides, Dorothy is em-

powering herself by cultivating the virtues of intelligence, compassion, and courage.
7. Baum, *The Wizard of Oz*, p. 17.
8. In the movie version of *The Wizard of Oz*, Dorothy's shoes are red.
9. We can draw another parallel between Dorothy's healing journey and that of the ancient Athenians. The Silver Shoes—symbol of understanding—help Dorothy heal. For the ancient Athenians, self-understanding was also the healing force. On the wall of the entrance hall to the temple at Delphi was inscribed the dictum, Know Thyself, which guided the worshipers of Apollo—and which became the cornerstone of modern psychotherapy.
10. Baum, *The Wizard of Oz*, p. 32.
11. Ibid., p. 55.
12. Ibid., p. 16.
13. Ibid., pp. 89–90.
14. Ibid., p. 163.
15. Ibid., p. 134.
16. Ibid., p. 187.
17. Ibid., pp. 211–213.
18. Ibid., p. 195.
19. Ibid., p. 198.

## Chapter 6

1. Irvin D. Yalom, *Existential Psychotherapy* (New York: Basic Books, 1980), p. 373.
2. Anaïs Nin, *Seduction of the Minotaur* (Athens, Ohio: Swallow Press, 1974), p. 531.
3. Judith Viorst, *Necessary Losses* (New York: Fawcett Gold Medal, 1986), pp. 75–76.
4. See Bessel A. van der Kolk, "The Compulsion to Repeat Trauma, Re-enactment, Revictimization, and Masochism," *Treatment of Victims of Sexual Abuse*, vol. 12, no. 2 (1989), pp. 389–411. In this review article, van der Kolk shows how trauma is repeated on behavioral, emotional, physiologic, and neuro-endocrinologic levels.
5. Erich Fromm, *The Art of Loving* (New York: Harper & Brothers, 1956), p. 34.
6. Wayne Phillips, M.D., Ph.D., who directs the center for victims of trauma at Centennial Peaks Hospital, Louisville, Colorado, tells me that there is accumulating clinical evidence that psychotherapists who seduce clients were often victims of childhood abuse.

7. Cited in Louise Bernikow, *Among Women* (New York: Harper & Row, 1981), p. 135.

8. Yalom, *Existential Psychotherapy*, p. 406.

9. According to Heinz Kohut, there are three types of relationship that lead to a cohesive and strong sense of self: relationships that provide affirming and confirming responses (mirroring relationships); relationships that allow one to feel connected to an idealized person (idealized relationships); and relationships that allow one to experience an essential alikeness with another valued person (twinship or alter-ego relationships). If one type of relationship is underdeveloped, a person can compensate by developing another type. (My gratitude to Ivan Miller, Ph.D., for synthesizing Kohut's work and providing a useful model of the sources of self-esteem.)

10. Reynolds Price, *Kate Vaiden* (New York: Atheneum, 1986), pp. 32–33.

## Chapter 7

1. *Red and Orange Hills*, 1938; *Red Hills and Bones*, 1941; *Cliffs Beyond Abiquiu*, 1943; *Red and Yellow Cliffs*, 1940.

2. Barbara G. Walker, *The Woman's Encyclopedia of Myths and Secrets* (New York: Harper & Row, 1983), p. 1066.

3. Anne Morrow Lindbergh, *Gift from the Sea* (New York: Vintage Books, 1978), p. 16.

4. Lisa Collier Cool, "How Does a Garden Grow," *Lears*, July-August 1989, pp. 28–29.

5. Ibid., p. 29.

6. Ibid.

7. William Wordsworth, "Tintern Abby," *William Wordsworth*, edited by Jonathan Wordsworth (Cambridge: Cambridge University Press, 1985), p. 38.

8. Georgia O'Keeffe, *Georgia O'Keeffe* (New York: Viking, 1976), p. 22.

9. Merlin Stone, *Ancient Mirrors of Womanhood* (Boston: Beacon Press, 1979), p. 292.

10. See Evelyn Bassoff, *Mothers and Daughters: Loving and Letting Go* (New York: New American Library, 1988), pp. 10–12, for further discussion.

11. Marie-Louise von Franz, *The Feminine in Fairytales* (Dallas, Tex.: Spring Publications, 1972), p. 86.

12. L. Frank Baum, *The Wizard of Oz* (New York: Ballantine Books, 1979), p. 4.

13. Alice Koller, *An Unknown Woman* (Toronto: Bantam, 1983), pp. 138–139.
14. J. E. Cirlot, *A Dictionary of Symbols* (New York: Philosophical Library, 1962), p. 145.
15. Marshall H. Klaus and John H. Kennel, *Maternal Infant Bonding* (Saint Louis: Mosby, 1976), p. 11.
16. After sending a copy of this chapter to my editor, Alexia Dorszynski, in New York, I was delighted to receive the following communication from her: "I think you should know that the gardens at Fort Tryon Park are still there, lovingly tended by volunteer gardeners."

## Chapter 8

1. See Lesley Dormen and Peter Edidin, "Original Spin," *Psychology Today*, July-August 1989, pp. 47–52.
2. I am reminded of lines from May Sarton's journal, *At Seventy* (New York: Norton, 1984): "The hardest thing we are asked to do in this world is remain aware of suffering. . . . Every human instinct is to turn away. Not see," p. 232.
3. C. J. Jung. *The Transcendent Function: Collected Works*, VIII (London: 1969), p. 73. Cited in Anthony Storr, *Solitude: A Return to the Self* (New York: Free Press, 1988), pp. 197–198.
4. May Sarton, *Writings on Writing* (Orono, Maine: Puckerbrush Press, 1980), p. 72.
5. Ibid.
6. The concept of a "false self" was first elaborated by Donald W. Winnicott.
7. Cited in Tillie Olsen, *Silences* (New York: Dell, 1965), p. 173.
8. Ibid., p. 208.
9. Cited in Storr, *Solitude*, p. 16.
10. Anne Morrow Lindbergh, *Gift from the Sea* (New York: Vintage Books, 1978), p. 42.
11. L. Frank Baum, *The Wizard of Oz* (New York: Ballantine Books, 1979), pp. 6–7.
12. Sarton, *Writings on Writing*, p. 11.
13. I discovered this quotation in Marion Woodman, *The Pregnant Virgin, A Process of Psychological Transformation* (Toronto: Inner City Books, 1985), p. 72.
14. Rollo May, *The Courage to Create* (New York: Norton, 1975), p. 46.
15. Baum, *The Wizard of Oz*, p. 17.
16. Cited in Alexandra Towle, ed., *Mothers* (New York: Simon & Schuster, 1988), p. 102.

## Chapter 9

1. C. J. Jung, *The Archetypes in the Collective Unconscious. Collected Works of C. J. Jung,* Vol. 9, Part 1, Bollingen Series (Princeton: Princeton University Press, 1959), p. 189.
2. There is some research evidence that people who survived the Holocaust tend to be emotionally distant as parents. See Susan L. Rose and John Garske, "Family Environment, Adjustment, and Coping Among Children of Holocaust Survivors: A Comparative Investigation," *American Journal of Orthopsychiatry,* vol. 57 (1987), pp. 332–344.
3. L. Frank Baum, *The Wizard of Oz* (New York: Ballantine, 1979), p. 169.
4. Tamar Lewin, "Aging Parents: Women's Burden Grows," *New York Times,* November 14, 1989, Section A, p. 1.
5. Evelyn Bassoff, *Mothers and Daughters: Loving and Letting Go* (New York: New American Library, 1988), p. 235.
6. In *The Wizard of Oz,* Baum writes that as Dorothy whirls through the air on her way home to Kansas, her Silver Shoes fall off and are lost in the desert forever. For the longest time, I could not make sense of this. "Why," I wondered "would Dorothy lose the symbol of her self-understanding?" My friend Ben Eilbott helped me understand that we cannot continue to wear our old shoes, which become too comfortable. True growing requires that we continually expand our self-awareness—that we are willing to modify our beliefs and ideas about the world. Figuratively speaking, we must be willing to try on new shoes, even if they are at first somewhat stiff and uncomfortable.
7. Baum, *The Wizard of Oz,* pp. 217–219.

# BIBLIOGRAPHY

Appleton, William. *Fathers and Daughters*. New York: Berkeley, 1984.

Arcana, Judith. *Our Mothers' Daughters*. Berkeley: Shameless Hussy Press, 1979.

Bassoff, Bruce. *Back Through the Glass*, © Bruce Bassoff, 1988.

Bassoff, Evelyn Silten. *Mothers and Daughters: Loving and Letting Go*. New York: New American Library, 1988.

Baum, L. Frank. *The Wizard of Oz*. New York: Ballantine, 1979, first published by Contemporary Books, 1956.

Beauvoir, Simone de. *The Second Sex*, translated and edited by H. M. Parshley. New York: Knopf, 1953.

Benjamin, Jessica. *The Bonds of Love: Psychoanalysis, Feminism, and the Problem of Domination*. New York: Pantheon, 1988.

Bernard, Jesse. *The Future of Motherhood*. New York: Penguin, 1974.

Bernikow, Louise. *Among Women*. New York: Harper & Row, 1981.

Bettelheim, Bruno. *The Uses of Enchantment*. New York: Vintage, 1977.

Bloomfield, Harold H., with Leonard Felder. *Making Peace with Your Parents*. New York: Ballantine, 1983.

Brothers Grimm. *Grimm's Fairy Tales*, translated by E. V. Lucas, Lucy Crane, and Martin Edwards. New York: Grosset & Dunlap, 1945.

Buber, Martin. *I and Thou*. New York: Scribner, 1970.

Cahill, Susan (ed.) *Mothers, Memories, Dreams and Reflections by Literary Daughters*. New York: New American Library, 1988.

Caplan, Paula. *Don't Blame Mother*. New York: Harper & Row, 1989.

Carlson, Kathie. *In Her Image: The Unhealed Daughter's Search for Her Mother*. Boston: Shambala, 1989.

Chernin, Kim. *In My Mother's House*. New York: Harper & Row, 1983.

———. *The Hungry Self: Women, Eating, and Identity.* New York: Harper & Row, 1986.

———. *Reinventing Eve: Modern Woman in Search of Herself.* New York: Harper & Row, 1988.

Cirlot, J. E. *A Dictionary of Symbols.* New York: Philosophical Library, 1962.

Colette. *My Mother's House and Sido,* translated by Una Vicenzo Troubridge and Enid McLeod. New York: Farrar, Straus and Giroux, 1953.

Demetrakopulos, Stephanie. *Listening to Our Bodies: The Rebirth of Feminine Wisdom.* Boston: Beacon, 1983.

DeSalvo, Louise. *Virginia Woolf: The Impact of Childhood Sexual Abuse on Her Life and Work.* Boston: Beacon, 1989.

Dinnerstein, Dorothy. *The Mermaid and the Minotaur.* New York: Harper & Row, 1976.

Dormen, Lesley, and Peter Edidin. "Original Spin," *Psychology Today,* July–August 1989, pp. 47–52.

Dowling, Colette. *Perfect Women.* New York: Summit, 1988.

Ehrenreich, Barbara, and Deirdre English. *For Her Own Good.* New York: Anchor Press/Doubleday, 1979.

Eichenbaum, Luise, and Susie Orbach. *Between Women.* New York: Viking, 1988.

Fischer, Lucy Rose. *Linked Lives: Adult Daughters and Their Mothers.* New York: Harper & Row, 1986.

Forward, Susan. *Toxic Parents.* New York: Bantam, 1989.

Fraiberg, Selma. *Every Child's Birthright: In Defense of Mothering.* Toronto: Bantam, 1977.

Frankl, Viktor E. *The Doctor and the Soul,* translated by Richard Winston and Clara Winston, New York: Vintage, 1973.

———. *Man's Search for Meaning.* Boston: Beacon, 1959.

Friday, Nancy. *My Mother/My Self.* New York: Dell, 1977.

———. *Jealousy.* Toronto: Bantam, 1985.

Friedan, Betty. *The Feminine Mystique.* New York: Dell, 1984.

Fromm, Erich. *The Art of Loving.* New York: Harper & Brothers, 1956.

Geist, Richard A. "Therapeutic Dilemmas in the Treatment of Anorexia Nervosa: A Self-Psychological Perspective." *Theory and Treatment of Anorexia and Bulimia,* edited by S. W. Emmett. New York: Brunner/Mazel, 1985.

Gornick, Vivian. *Fierce Attachments.* New York: Simon & Schuster, 1987.

Goudeket, Maurice. *Close to Colette.* New York: Farrar, Straus and Giroux, 1957.

Hackl, Erich. *Aurora's Motive: A Novel,* translated by Edna McCown. New York: Knopf, 1989.

Hammer, Emanuel H. "Artistic Creativity: Giftedness or Sickness." *The Arts in Psychotherapy,* vol. 2 (1975), pp. 173–175.

Hellman, Lillian. *An Unfinished Woman: A Memoir.* New York: Little, Brown, 1970.

Herman, Judith Lewis, with Lisa Hirschman. *Father-Daughter Incest.* Cambridge: Harvard University Press, 1981.

Jung, C. J. *The Archetypes of the Collective Unconscious. Collected Works of C. J. Jung,* Vol. 9, Part 1, translated by R.F.C. Hull. Princeton: Princeton University Press, Bollingen Series, 1959.

Kaledin, Eugenia. *Mothers and More: American Women in the 1950's.* Boston: Twayne, 1984.

Kaplan, Louise J. *Oneness and Separateness: From Infant to Individual.* New York: Simon & Schuster, 1978.

Klaus, Marshall H., and John H. Kennel. *Maternal Infant Bonding.* Saint Louis: Mosby, 1976.

Klinnert, Mary, Joseph Campos, and Robert Emde. "The Role of Maternal Facial Signaling on the Visual Cliff," *Developmental Psychology,* vol. 21 (1985), pp. 195–200.

Kolbenschlag, Madonna. *Lost in the Land of Oz.* San Francisco: Harper & Row, 1988.

Kohut, Heinz. *The Analysis of the Self.* New York: International Universities Press, 1971.

———. *The Restoration of the Self.* New York: International Universities Press, 1977.

———. *How Does Analysis Cure?* Posthumously edited by Arnold Goldberg with Paul E. Stepansky. Chicago: University of Chicago Press, 1984.

Koller, Alice. *An Unknown Woman.* Toronto: Bantam, 1983.

Lamb, Michael E. (ed.) *The Role of the Father in Child Development.* New York: Wiley, 1981.

Lao-tzu. *Tao Te Ching,* translated by Herrymon Maurer. New York: Schocken, 1985.

Leonard, Linda Schierse. *The Wounded Woman.* Boulder: Shambala, 1983.

Lewin, Tamar. "Aging Parents: Women's Burden Grows," *New York Times,* November 14, 1989, Section A, page 1.

Lindbergh, Anne Morrow. *Gift from the Sea.* New York: Vintage, 1978.

McCarthy, Mary. *The Group.* New York: Harcourt, Brace, and World, 1954.

Masterson, James E. *The Real Self.* New York: Brunner/Mazel, 1985.

May, Rollo. *The Courage to Create.* New York: Norton, 1975.

Miller, Alice. *The Drama of the Gifted Child,* translated by Ruth Ward. New York: Basic Books, 1981.

———. *For Your Own Good,* translated by Hildegarde and Hunter Hannum. New York: Farrar, Straus and Giroux, 1983.

———. *Thou Shalt Not Be Aware,* translated by Hildegarde and Hunter Hannum. New York: New American Library, 1984.

Miller, Ivan. "Interpersonal Vulnerability and Narcissism: A Conceptual Continuum for Understanding and Treating Narcissistic Psychopathology." Unpublished manuscript, 1990.

Moore, Susanna. *The Whiteness of Bones.* New York: Doubleday, 1989.

Morrison, Toni. *Beloved.* New York: New American Library, 1987.

Munro, Alice. *Dance of the Happy Shades.* New York: McGraw Hill, 1968.

Neumann, Erich. *The Great Mother: An Analysis of the Archetype,* translated by Ralph Mannheim. Bollingen Series XLVII. Princeton: Princeton University Press, 1963.

Nin, Anaïs. *The Diary of Anaïs Nin,* edited by Gunther Stuhlmann. Athens, Ohio: Swallow Press, 1966.

———. *Seduction of the Minotaur.* Athens, Ohio: Swallow Press, 1974.

O'Keeffe, Georgia. *Georgia O'Keeffe.* New York: Viking, 1976.

Olsen, Tillie. *Tell Me a Riddle.* New York: Dell, 1960.

———. *Silences.* New York: Dell, 1965.

———. *Mother to Daughter, Daughter to Mother.* New York: Feminist Press, 1984.

Payne, Karen (ed.). *Between Ourselves: Letters Between Mothers and Daughters.* Boston: Houghton Mifflin, 1983.

Phelps, Elizabeth Stuart Lyon. *The Story of Avis,* edited by Carol Farley Kessler. New Brunswick, N. J.: Rutgers University Press, 1985.

Price, Reynolds. *Kate Vaiden.* New York: Atheneum, 1986.

Reidar, Th. Christiansen (ed.). "Mophead," *Folktales of Norway,* translated by Pat Shaw Iverson. Chicago: University of Chicago Press, 1964.

Rich, Adrienne. "Phantasia for Elvira Shatayev," *The Dream of a Common Language*. New York: Norton, 1978.

Rose, Susan L., and John Garske. "Family Environment, Adjustment, and Coping Among Children of Holocaust Survivors: A Comparative Investigation," *American Journal of Orthopsychiatry*, vol. 57 (1987), pp. 332–344.

Sarton, May. *Writings on Writing*. Orono, Maine: Puckerbrush Press, 1980.

Schreiner, Olive. "From Three Dreams in a Desert," *A Track to the Water's Edge: The Olive Schreiner Reader*, edited by Howard Thurman. New York: Harper & Row, 1973.

Schwartz-Salant, Nathan. *Narcissism and Character Transformation*. Toronto: Inner City Books, 1982.

Sendak, Maurice. *Outside Over There*. New York: Harper & Row, 1981.

Steinem, Gloria. "Ruth's Song (Because She Could Not Sing It)," *Outrageous Acts and Everyday Rebellions*. New York: Holt, Rinehart & Winston, 1983.

Stern, Daniel N. *The First Relationship*. Cambridge: Harvard University Press, 1977.

———. *The Interpersonal World of the Infant*. New York: Basic Books, 1985.

Stone, Merlin. *When God Was a Woman*. New York: Harcourt Brace Jovanovich, 1978.

———. *Ancient Mirrors of Womanhood*. Boston: Beacon Press, 1979.

Storr, Anthony. *Solitude: A Return to the Self*. New York: Free Press, 1988.

Thomas, Marlo. *Free to be . . . you and me*, edited by Carole Hart. New York: McGraw Hill, 1974.

Towle, Alexandra (ed.). *Mothers*. New York: Simon & Schuster, 1988.

Vanderbilt, Gloria. *Woman to Woman*. New York: Doubleday, 1979.

van der Kolk, Bessel A. "The Trauma Spectrum: The Interaction of Biological and Social Events in the Genesis of the Trauma Response," *Journal of Traumatic Stress*, vol. 1, no. 3 (1988), pp. 273–290.

———. "The Compulsion to Repeat Trauma, Re-enactment, Revictimization, and Masochism," *Treatment of Victims of Sexual Abuse*, vol. 12, no. 2 (1989), pp. 389–411.

Viorst, Judith. *Necessary Losses*. New York: Fawcett Gold Medal, 1986.

von Franz, Marie-Louise. *The Feminine in Fairytales*. Dallas, Tex.: Spring Publications, 1972.

Walker, Barbara. *The Woman's Encyclopedia of Myths and Secrets*. New York: Harper & Row, 1983.

Whitfield, Charles L. *Healing the Child Within*. Deerfield Beach, Fla.: Health Communications, 1987.

Winnicott, Donald W. "Primary Maternal Preoccupation," *Collected Papers*. New York: Basic Books, 1956.

————. "The Theory of Parent-Infant Relationship," *International Journal of Psychoanalysis*, vol. 41 (1960), pp. 585–595.

————. *The Child, the Family, and the Outside World*. New York: Penguin, 1964.

Woodman, Marion. *The Pregnant Virgin, A Process of Psychological Transformation*. Toronto: Inner City Books, 1985.

Woolf, Virginia. *To the Lighthouse*. New York: Harcourt Brace Jovanovich, 1927.

————. "Professions for Women," *The Death of the Moth and Other Essays*. New York: Hogarth Press and Harcourt Brace Jovanovich, 1942.

————. *A Cockney's Farming Experiences and the Experiences of a Paterfamilias*, edited by Suzanne Heinig. San Diego: San Diego State University Press, 1972.

————. "A Sketch of the Past," *Moments of Being, Unpublished Autobiographical Writings*, edited by Jeanne Shulkind. New York: Harcourt Brace Jovanovich, 1985.

Wordsworth, William. "Tintern Abby," *William Wordsworth*, edited by Jonathan Wordsworth. Cambridge: Cambridge University Press, 1985.

Yalom, Irvin D. *The Theory and Practice of Group Psychotherapy*. New York: Basic Books, 1975.

————. *Existential Psychotherapy*. New York: Basic Books, 1980.

Zimmer, Heinrich. *The King and the Corpse*, edited by Joseph Campbell. Bollingen Series XI. New York: Pantheon, 1948.

# INDEX